W. Lawrence Lipton

presents

President Ted Cruz

W. Lawrence Lipton

presents

President Ted Cruz

The 2016 Election and America's Future

Copyright © 2013

Books may be ordered through booksellers or by contacting:

www.createspace.com/4548640
www.Amazon.com

———————

CreateSpace Title ID: <4548640>

Jacked Design by Guebres Studios

ISBN-13: 978-1494321697 (sc)
ISBN-10: 1494321696 (ebk)

Printed in the United States of America
CreateSpace rev. date: 12/01/2013

<u>ACKNOWLEDGMENTS</u>

To those who would change America.
This is your time in history.
To encourage a thing,
First lie about it;
Then prohibit it.
Discriminate,
Stereotype,
Devalue.
Ignore the needs of your neighbor.
Don't define your terminology.
They will assume a meaning.
Until you destroy them,
Then see their error.
Always enrich those who are rich.
Always empower the powerful.
Never seek the facts.
Accept assertion,
On faith.
Empower proven liars.
Empower all inconsistency.
Empower the proven deceivers.
Let others make all your decisions.
If you are not for yourself,
Who will be for you?
If not now, when?

CHAPTERS

Introduction

Imagine, if you can, that Senator Ted Cruz ran for President in 2016.

Picture in your mind someone who resembles the actor-comedian Bill Murray, and whose approach to political situations resembles events in the 1993 film *"Groundhog Day"* – the movie in which Murray finds himself in a time loop, repeating the same day over and over. Only in our scenario, our protagonist is continually attacking a piece of legislation called *The Affordable Care Act* (ACA), but which has come to be referred to as *Obamacare*. He might even have a wife who approximates a blond version of Andie MacDowell.

In our scenario, what is essentially a marketplace summary of all available healthcare insurance offers, is confused with the actual services which constitute health care. As a result, the nation is placed in a potentially self-destructive time-loop which requires it to revisit the same issue, as new knowledge or information is added or learned. The problem arises as some characters blindly repeat their behavior and reject what is emerging; these character constitute the Tea Party voter base.

By focusing attention on the programming problems inherent it a broad-based consumer marketing website, people are distracted from the reality that they, like employers who want to buy healthcare plans for their workers, could easily go through an insurance company or agent, rather than through any government website. Moreover, the focus ignores the primary fact that the target beneficiaries of the reform are people living at, or below, poverty level, and therefore are not likely to have the necessary internet access to avail themselves of the website.

Obviously, it is highly unlikely that the attack on ACA will sustain itself into, much less past, the November 2014 election cycle. Therefore, as a 2016 issue, at best, it will only reflect upon the intellectual level of those who engaged in the October 2013 governmental shutdown, and their willingness to plunge the nation into default on its lawful debts – over what is essentially a government funded marketing resource for various private insurers specializing in Health care Insurance.

In dealing with the sustainability of attacks on ACA, it is necessary to concede that Republicans have launched countless legal and political challenges to the law since its passage in 2010. Moreover, as I write these words, there is at least one case – *Hobby Lobby vs. The Affordable Care Act* – in which the family owners of a corporate arts and crafts chain is seeking to deny their employees the healthcare plan birth control benefits option.

The basis for the Hobby Lobby case is the Religious Freedom Restoration Act, enacted in 1993 to protect "a person's exercise of religion" from government intrusion.

The U.S. solicitor general's office has asserted that a victory for the company transforms the *Religious Freedom Restoration Act* "from a shield for individuals and religious institutions into a sword used to deny employees of for-profit commercial enterprises the benefits and protections of generally applicable laws."

In this instance, the Green family, which owns Hobby Lobby, is seeking to deny coverage to roughly 13,000 employees and their families. Obviously, if they succeed, they open the door to challenges of any and all portions of every federal law which can be construed to challenge a religious conviction – certain Mormon groups could challenge monogamy laws, or all health care could be denied based on a belief in witchcraft and demons as the source of illness. Possibilities which are not outlandish within the context of legal theory under which the *Religious Freedom Restoration Act* is currently being invoke.

As the matter stood, in December 2013, the lower court had ruled in favor of Hobby Lobby, and the Tenth Circuit Court of Appeals held that the definition of "person" under the law includes corporations regardless of their profit-making status. Furthermore, the court recognized that the statutory fines, associated with their not seeking to compromise their religious belief, would force Hobby Lobby [the Green family] to incur a substantial economic burden.

Unlike other attacks on the ACA, the Hobby Lobby action has managed to find a possible legal theory which capitalizes on the vague legal assertion that a corporation is, under existing statutory terminology, a "person." But that theory can only persist if Hobby Lobby is deemed a "person" who is part of the Green family, and shares their religious convictions.

But, as with every other legal problem, it deals with a system which wields a double edged sword – in this instance, one which could shatter the liability protection afforded those who incorporate their businesses.

As it has been put, one can not argue both that a corporation is indistinguishable from it's owner for First Amendment/religious viewpoint, and then argue that the same owner is shielded from any personal liabilities corporate torts because the corporation is a separate entity.

From the Hobby Lobby case, to the October Shutdown, we are faced with draconian consequences from those who oppose the principal of providing "Good Samaritan" style healthcare to those who lack the means to provide it for themselves.

Of course, taking a "Good Samaritan" approach would infer some Christian values were in play – and nothing in recognized scripture stands against abortion, which was a common practice in the first century. This is especially true of the Talmud (Yevamot 69b) which holds the fetus is just water for the first 40 days.

Though, as was pointed out in the 2012 book, *Saint Paul's Joke*, for gentiles (non-Hebrews), not having children, or engaging in any act which might produce them, was the Christian ideal.

St. Paul's writings are explicit in the fact that they require his Gentile converts adhere to all the Hebrew laws – which might raise valid questions as to religious convictions held by the Green family. Again, some concepts and assertions wield a double edged sword.

In the case of the Tea Party, and Ted Cruz as its Presidential representative, we are faced with a few problems of definition as allied by his followers to Barack Obama and to Ted Cruz. These can include definitions of honesty, and their very Constitutional right to hold Presidential Office.

In many regards the idea of a President Ted Cruz is the thing immigrant dreams are made of; it is the dream, which came true, when Barack Obama was elected President.

In both we see strong parallels:

1. An immigrant comes to America and gains a quality education;

2. They meet and married "native born" American woman;

3. They father a son who becomes an attorney with a degree from Harvard Law, and who then become politicians who rises to elective office in the nation's capitol, Senators – Cruz from Texas; Obama from Illinois.

4. In both cases, the parents divorced – Obama's when he was a toddler; Cruz's when he was in Law School.

5. Both me attended Harvard Law, where Obama became an editor of the Harvard Law Review, and first black president of the Harvard Law Review; while Cruz was editor of the Harvard Law Review, and executive editor of the Harvard Journal of Law and Public Policy, and a founding editor of the Harvard Latino Law Review.

6. Both men graduated Harvard Law *magna cum laude*.

7. All other things being equal, the fact that their mothers were American citizens would mean, regardless of where they were born, both Barack and Ted were entitled to American citizenship.

The only real difference between the two? Barack was born in Hawaii, two years after it became a state, while Rafael Edward Cruz was born in Calgary, Alberta, Canada. Thus, Barack entered the world as a 'natural born' American, and Ted a Canadian.

And therein lies the rub, the differences in how the American Dream can be fulfilled. Can a first generation Cuban-American-Canadian achieve what has been accomplished by a first generation African-American-American?

Could Rafael Edward 'Ted' Cruz become the head of the most powerful nation in history, and reign as leader of the 'Free World'?

PRESIDENT TED CRUZ
Is it a possibility?

The American Constitution is explicit as to the qualifications for those who would be its leader: Article II, Section 1, "No Person except a natural born Citizen, or a Citizen of the United States, at the time of the Adoption of this Constitution, shall be eligible to the Office of President; ..."

Because the US Constitution prevents foreign-born citizens from holding the nation's top job, actor and former California Governor Arnold Schwarzenegger – who, as Governor of California, built a favorable constituency, and one which would support his bid for president, has reportedly been talking openly about working on getting the constitutional rules changed so he can run for president in 2016. He is ready to file legal paperwork to challenge the rules."

Were that Amendment process to move forward, he would need a two-thirds majority in the House and the Senate before any change could be put to the States for their two-thirds ratification. And while sufficient people might not support Schwarzenegger's bid, those who support Cruz certainly join in.

Once ratified, the Amendment would negate any possible Constitutional objection to a Ted Cruz candidacy. Moreover, if the process were to fail, Schwarzenegger's organization would have sole liability for the failure, and not The Tea Party.

Given the possibility of a third party initiated Constitutional Amendment, there is the possibility that Ted Cruz could be eligible to be elected President in 2016. Even without such an amendment, any definition either enacted by Congress, or, through some legal challenge, imposed by the Supreme Court, could define 'a natural born American' as being one whose mother is American.

Now some would ask why I specify 'mother' and not 'father.' But that is something which will be discussed later in this book. For now, it is sufficient to hold that the term 'natural born' has a degree of legal wiggle-room because it is a terminology from the latter eighteenth century which does not allow for the scientific-medical realities of the twenty-first century which can see someone in New York City within twenty-four hours of their being in Tokyo, Japan.

When the Founders drafted the Constitution the words of Article II, Section 1, there were numerous differences. The United States consisted of Thirteen former British Colonies on the Atlantic seaboard; slavery was legal, and, for purposes of the census, slaves counted as fractional people; and the words 'natural born', if they were considered in Shakespearean terms – "*NOT of woman born*" (Macbeth: Act 5, Scene 8) – could reasonably exclude anyone born by Cesarean section.

If a President elect is "*NOT of woman born*," how could they possibly be considered "*a natural born Citizen*"?

We have statutes which define a citizen for the purpose of holding a passport, or having the right to vote, but we cannot rely on statutes governing citizenship to answer the question of what "*a natural born Citizen*" means in this day and age.

However, it must be noted, as you can imagine, the issue of a Cesarean section, in "*a natural born Citizen*" context, has been spoken of and deemed to mean the words '*natural born*' has nothing to do with the mode of delivery. Rather it refers to where he was born and the possible influence of who his parents were, or where they were citizens and why a child was born where they were.

Some scholars have labeled the Natural-Born Citizen Clause the "Constitution's worst provision." On one level, their assertion is predicated on the inference naturalized Americans are less loyal than native-born citizens. But, as derogatory as that might seem, a more rational justification for the clause would come from exclusion of any who might be foreign agents, or nobility who will then assert Royalist authority over the military.

Even today, with stories of sleeper-agents who function as normal everyday citizens until they are activated, we need to be aware of external influences.

Imagine if Bismarck's Germany had instituted some similar provision in the 1860's. Austria was not Germany, so Austrians were not, nor could they claim to be, *'natural born Germans'*. Now consider that Adolf Hitler was born in Austria, thirty years later.

In World War I, Hitler volunteered to serve in the Bavarian Army as an Austrian citizen. Thus, he could not claim German citizenship through military service, which is a route that opened the road to American citizenship for many foreign born men. But, even that would not make them eligible to hold office as President or vice-President.

If we look at Hitler's professional background, we discover a highly intelligent man – whose DNA shows he came from the same North African Berber line as Albert Einstein – but he had little formal education and no clearly defined career prospects. Surviving works show that he was a fairly accomplished artist, who might well have had a career in art. But he decided to remain in the military.

After the war, Hitler was assigned the role of intelligence agent for a reconnaissance commando unit; his assignment was to infiltrate and report on the activities of the German Workers' Party (DAP). Part of his training, and apparently a natural skill, lay in his ability to influence others. But, as it turned out, while conducting his DAP duties, Hitler was drawn to the ideas of DAO founder, Anton Drexler. Those ideas were basically anti-Marxist socialism, combined with an anti-capitalist, antisemitic nationalism.

In many way we seem similar patterns emerge in the use of "socialist" to describe biblical commandments to care for the sick, widowed, orphaned, or elderly. And we see the anti-capitalist ideas in the granting of special interests preferred tax rates which then negatively impact free market commerce through a distortion of economic factors which influence the ability to compete on a level playing field.

Imagine a world in which Hitler's birthplace would have been a basis for preventing his election as Chancellor, or Prime Minister, of Germany. As you think about that, consider that effectively, the Chancellor, in a Parliamentary System, serves the role of a nation's President. The existence of a 'natural born' clause, in the Germany equivalent of our Constitution, might have served to prevent the

Nazi party from gaining control, and thereby prevented World War II.

The idea someone can rise to the leadership of a nation only by being "*a natural born citizen*" of that nation is not a minor idea to be dismissed with ideas of disloyalty on the part of naturalized citizens. We can even play with the status of the German Chancellor at the time when Hitler came to power. But it is all too easy for us to create scenarios where foreign agents can not only rise to roles of influence, but, if allowed to rule, could bring down a nation.

Comically, such scenarios have already been created for us, and comprise a major element of fictional entertainment media. A nation can be destroyed, if you destroy its credit worthiness, in you manipulate events to undermine it reliability. For example, we now know that the non-aggression treaty Hitler entered into with Russia, was, in Hitler's mind, a sham to delay an inevitable conflict. We also know that al Qaeda has asserted its desire to see a Bankrupted America – something which could only happen if the "*full faith and credit*" of the nation were brought into question; that could best be achieved by a covert operative who acquired the power to veto any and all legislation having to do with monetary transactions, or the enforcement of treaties.

We know the concerns which existed when the American Constitution was drafted; we need go no further than the words of John Jay's July 25, 1787 letter to George Washington:

"Permit me to hint, whether it would be wise and seasonable to provide a strong check to the admission of Foreigners into the administration of our national Government; and to declare expressly that the Command in Chief of the American army shall not be given to nor devolve on, any but a natural born Citizen."

We would note there are two related provisions, first that the individual be at least thirty-five years of age, and that they have resided in the United States for fourteen years. Thus, if we say that any foreign-born children of citizen parents are also 'natural-born' United States citizens – as opposed to simply American citizens – then any child who spends the first twenty-one years of their life in a foreign jurisdiction, having received both a foreign education and indoctrination into a foreign culture, is qualified to be President.

That seems rather dangerous.

Once a law is changed, the door is opened to a cascade-effect of re-definitions. Every new definition brings a risk of activating the law of unintended consequences, so specificity – explicitly defined terms, boundaries, or limitations – becomes mandatory.

If America was Great Britain in an era when the British could say that the 'sun never set on the Empire', than the 1708 British law providing "foreign-born children of natural-born British subjects shall 'be deemed, adjudged and taken to be natural-born subjects of this kingdom, to all intents, constructions and purposes ...'" might be held valid in the United States. Similarly, the 1773 British law granting natural-born status to the grandchildren of natural-born subjects might also apply, and further distort who could hold the offices of President and vice-President. By logical extension, if the grandchildren are deemed 'natural born citizens,' than it follows that their grandchildren (who are the great-great grandchildren of the original individuals born in Great Britain) would also qualify.

Very quickly, all those with the slightest bit of imagination, would have realized that these British laws would eventually render the whole world subjects of the Queen (or King). Carrying this silly legalese a bit further, nearly every American is a dual national who holds British 'natural-born' citizenship. In Israel this would be the equivalent of return – though then we would need to consider that orthodox sects do hold that Jewishness is passed only through the mother (which is mentioned in a later chapter).

But our problem – if Ted Cruz is to be President and the Tea Party to gain national authority – is finding a compelling argument to disregard the dual facts that he was born in Canada to parents, only one of whom, his mother, was unquestionably a citizen.

Cruz's father, Evangelical Minister Rafael Cruz, was, at the time of Ted's birth, a Cuban national who apparently had not even begun the paperwork which would qualify him for naturalization as an America citizen.

8 USC Natural Born

George W. Romney, father of Mitt Romney, was born in Mexico, in 1907. At the time, his parents and maternal grandfather were serving as Mormon missionaries in Chihuahua. All were, apparently, natural born American citizens. In 1968, Romney became a Republican nominee for President, and had the effect of making a natural born Mexican the initial front runner in the process leading to occupancy of the highest office in the nation.

At no time does there appear to have been any challenge regarding his Constitutional eligibility to be a candidate, or, if successful, to hold office. A fact which provides a compelling basis to assert that either the Democrats or Republicans maintained any basis to hold that the child of two American citizens – regardless of the geographic location of his birth – could be held ineligible to be President.

That does not mean that a challenge might not have been raised, had Romney not lost the nomination to Richard M. Nixon – who had been the Republican candidate defeated by John F. Kennedy.

It is also worth noting that, when Kennedy was nominated, there were many who attacked the fact he was an Irish Catholic from Boston, allegedly a papal stooge, and servant to the Vatican bureaucracy.

Since we know the level of the debate aimed at Kennedy, it stands to reason that, had George Romney been nominated, his status as a natural born Mexican would have become an issue for him. Had that happened, we would now have some form of precedent to use in a Constitutional debate over Ted Cruz's status as a natural born Canadian – with a mother who is a natural born American citizen, and a father who is both a natural born Cuban, and a former Castro Revolutionary Freedom Fighter.

We already know that there is a statutory INA provisions which grant citizenship to the children who are born outside American territory, and who have a parent, or parents, who hold

American citizenship.

As an alternative, to one born in a neighboring, but foreign, country, let's consider the case of John McCain.

McCain was born in the Panama Canal Zone on August 29, 1936. The Panama Canal Zone was not a proper territory of the United States, rather it was administered under a 1903 treaty with Panama.

In accordance with 8 USC § 1403 - Persons born in the Canal Zone or Republic of Panama on or after February 26, 1904, (a) "… whose father or mother or both at the time of the birth of such person was or is a citizen of the United States, is declared to be a citizen of the United States."

However, we have section (b) "… whose father or mother or both at the time of the birth of such person was or is a citizen of the United States employed by the Government of the United States or by the Panama Railroad Company, or its successor in title, is declared to be a citizen of the United States."

Two clauses which essentially state the same thing. Why say it twice? While one would need to examine the debate and discussion associated with the law, the second clause would seem to infer a different citizenship for those who were born in Panama because their parents were government employees; thus the child was born there because their parents were on official government business. That being the case, a child could not rightfully be denied their status as "*a natural born Citizen.*"

The U.S. Senate voted a non-binding resolution, "S.Res.511 - A resolution recognizing that John Sidney McCain, III, is a natural born citizen." On 30 April 2008, the resolution was passed without amendment, and, by definition – effectively in accordance with the meaning behind 8 USC § 1403b – John McCain was defined to be "*a natural born Citizen*" as meant by in Article II, Section 1. This then infers that anyone born American controlled territory while their citizen parent was on official government business, qualifies as "*a natural born Citizen*" and therefore is eligible to hold elected office as either President or vice-President.

One of the objections raised to the Senate interpretation of 8 USC §1403b included the fact that the law was not enacted until a year after John McCain was born. However, the law was clearly a retroactive clarification of status which was intended to extend to the date of the original treaty; therefore it becomes a Constitutional definition with regard to the meaning behind the wording of the Fourteenth Amendment, "all persons born or naturalized in the United States, and subject to the jurisdiction thereof, are citizens of the United States." Specifically affecting the use of the words, "the United States", in the context of "subject to the jurisdiction thereof" – you are "*a natural born Citizen*" if you are born within territory under the sovereign jurisdiction of the United States.

By extension, anyone born in an American Embassy, or on a foreign military base, would be both a citizen and "*a natural born Citizen*", if one or both parents were already citizens. This would then exclude any individuals of non-citizens parents who might be born in an American facility in a foreign country, but include the children of Americans at the same facility.

8 USC §1401 defines citizenship, or "*a natural born Citizen,*" as anyone born inside the United States, who is also "subject to the jurisdiction" of the United States – thus excluding the children of foreign Diplomas, or others who enjoy diplomatic immunity from domestic laws.

The parents of Ted Cruz were NOT diplomats subject to the jurisdiction of the United States, the were private workers subject to Canadian authority and jurisdiction; therefore Ted Cruz is not "*a natural born Citizen*" within any logical argument which could be construed from the existing statutory definitions and requirements.

The Senate could pass a resolution which redefines the basis for 8 USC §1403a, and would open the door to any child/citizen of an American born overseas to being "*a natural born Citizen*", and after fourteen years of residency, qualified to be President.

CHAPTER I

The Tea Party

We have a world in which those who see someone successful, are not being inspired to achieve their own success, rather they seek to destroy the success of the other person. They seek to drag them down to their level, rather than raise themselves up.

This attitude has a corollary in that those who have achieved success step on the fingers of those climbing up, rather than offer a helping hand. We see this in those who attack welfare, those who seek to deprive the poor, the aged and the sick of assistance.

Of course the excuse they give is that those on assistance are too lazy to work, or help themselves. But those who make that assertion are also the ones who pay below subsistence wages, and are working to out-source the very jobs they claim the poor should be seeking.

What are the core principles of the Tea Party movement? If you ask their membership, or leaders, the response would include three elements: limited government, fiscal responsibility, and free enterprise.

But in areas with a large Latino population, and people who, like Ted Cruz's father, escaped Communist Cuba – many by illegally immigrating to the United States – the issue of immigrant amnesty is, because they can relate to it, deemed one of importance.

In Florida, 42 year-old Senator Marco Rubio, who was born in Miami, now dominates the potential 2016 GOP presidential field among Latinos, and has given a majority of Latinos an excuse to abandon their traditional Democratic affiliation to cross party lines and consider voting Republican.

However, were he to be pitted against Hillary Clinton, the same polling data indicates she would garner nearly two thirds of the Latino vote against any Republican.

As far as any Tea Party candidate is concerned, Rubio and Clinton represent a dual problem in securing the critical Latino vote – Ted Cruz may be Cuban on his father's side, but these voters are concerned with immigration reform, and the Roman Catholic Rubio voted for the Senate immigration-reform bill in June 2013, and now immigration reform has become the next major item on the Obama agenda.

In contrast to Rubio, Ted Cruz has consistently opposed the immigration bill, voting against its advancement in the Senate three times – apparently because, while it granted amnesty, it also failed to button down the border and so repeated a problem with the 1986 immigration law signed by President Ronald Reagan.

Whether the amnesty legalization means any formal status that allows a person to stay and work in the U.S., even temporarily, or a granting permanent legal residency, often referred to as a green card, was also somewhat uncertain in terms of the granting of a "registered provisional immigrant" status for those here illegally.

The Congressional Budget Office (CBO) held that provisional status and the blue card constitute legalization, or clear amnesty, for those who entered the United States illegally. For Cuban, many of whom know that their grandparents risked life and limb in leaky boats to reach Florida, the idea of being accepted has merit.

In explaining his position, Sen. Cruz said, "My point is very simple: what is the rush? ... The only explanation that makes sense is there are many senators in this body, perhaps on both sides of the aisle, that very much want a fig leaf. They want something that they can claim we are supporting border security when, in fact, this bill does not. ... Fundamentally, this is about political cover. It's not about solving the problem. It is an approach that says: I will gladly secure the border next Tuesday for legalization today."

So, from his statements, we can deduce that Cruz would not opposed a legalization bill, if it also dealt with closing the borders, or possibly allowed the borders to be a separate issue that is dealt with prior to any discussion of immigrant reform.

In many ways, Cruz is correct in asserting both the need for border security, and need to address it now – not at some vague future date. This matter has been dragging out since 1986, and, if you recall, we had a bit of an incident in September 2001 which might have been prevented if the nation had a better immigration policy and more secure borders. As 9/11 established, this so-called illegal immigration, or the granting of amnesty and formal status to those who, like most of our common ancestors, came to America to find freedom and a better life.

We need to focus on those whose arrival is for the transient purpose of murdering innocent people in the name of some group which prides itself on the murder of innocents.

The problem is, as we saw with the government shutdown, the Tea Party has well over a dozen Senators, and over a hundred Congressman, who will vote their agenda. That is clearly more than enough members of Congress to prepare and submit legislation which would secure the borders. Unfortunately, they seem to be limited by their ability to vote against legislation, without offering any constructive to address the objectives they assert.

If, in the context of Obamacare or Healthcare, we look back to the elements of limited government, fiscal responsibility, and free enterprise, we see an interesting conflict – one designated a Public Option.

A brainchild of Yale political scientist Jacob Hacker, the Public Option would allow those under age 65 to buy into Medicare. The free market, free enterprise, is based on the most efficient, most economical, most beneficial, offering being made available to the people, and allowing them to choose what they wish to buy.

The Public Option recognizes Medicare to be more efficient than comparable private sector insurance, and asserts that, over time, the Public Option would gradually drive out private insurance. Or, private insurance companies would find a means to become far more efficient and diligent in their delivery of their services.

Basically, the Public Option is free market enterprise without the bigotry which has marked all references made by professional nay-sayers when referring to government programs.

In many regards, Healthcare is like an Interstate Highway system where occasional tolls are utilized to cover immediate costs of borrowed capital. We need to ask why the highway system did no emerge through the private sector, and if the public would be willing to pay what would amount to a no investment annuity to the builder after the initial costs have been covered.

Society needs the type of connectivity which highways and roads provide – there is a clear free market need, which was once filled by the private sector's transcontinental rail system, why isn't the private sector providing it?

Society needs healthy workers. It does not need workers who are allowed to develop preventable catastrophic illness because they cannot pay for routine check-up due to the premiums associated with insuring against the catastrophic event which will follow. But it is by ignoring the routine, and covering the catastrophic, that the private companies make their money.

In many situations, the actuarial tables utilized by insurance companies are predicated on the fact you will die before making a claim – rendering all the premiums you paid unencumbered free profit. A reality that it is fiscally irresponsible to ignore, or fail to address.

That fiscal irresponsible is heightened by the fact that money diverted to premiums is unavailable for circulation in local consumer economies, and therefore unavailable for taxation – tax funds needed to cover deficit spending of the type which Reagan, Bush and Bush each used to double the Nation Debt during their respective terms in office.

To limit the scope of government, government should be restricted to engaging in the most efficient use of available funds; it should not be running deficits which necessitate increased taxation, without any increased services – which is what happens when funds go to pay foreign nations the interest on loans to cover deficits.

With their focus on limited government, fiscal responsibility, and free enterprise, what is the Tea Party offering as their program to provide consumers more after-tax disposable income?

If we think in term of 'free enterprise' – which carries with it the idea that the private sector can outperform the public one, the Tea Party orchestrated government shutdown in October 2013 can take on some rather interesting nuance.

Republican Tom Scully, principal health policy adviser under President George H. W. Bush, revealed, "Obamacare, was largely based on past Republican initiatives. If you took [Bush's] health plan and removed the label, you'd think it was Obamacare."

Scully helped formulate many past Republican initiatives — like the shift to a private-insurance program — that Obamacare has put into law, and reduces state costs by billions of dollars.

Under George W. Bush, Scully ran the Centers for Medicare and Medicaid Services and oversaw a host of proto-Obamacare reforms, like Medicare Part D, which introduced competition into the government-supported health care market.

Affordable Care Act is not a single payer socialist program. A point of indisputable fact: the ACA is a private sector controlled program which was originally proposed by Republican Conservative Ronald Reagan. Having failed to gain Congressional support, the program was redesigned for George H. W. Bush, then, once again, it was redrawn into its current form for President George W. Bush.

Each of those Republican Presidents was a strong supporter of the private sector, and their healthcare program was, as we see in the ACA, designed to increase the client base for private insurers. The fact that it utilized public subsidies does not detract from the reality that it is a privately operated, consumer based, program.

If we think in terms of the October shutdown and drive to defund the ACA, we find the nuance of a series of actions that are anti-capitalistic, anti-free market, or anti-free enterprise.

The private insurers stand to make a significant amount from the new customer base, and, assuming the risks are covered as the law requires, their profits will increase. So we must ask why the Tea Party is opposed to increased corporate profits – especially in an industry whose corporate profits are routinely invested in domestic fixed assets (real estate).

In theory, like Reagan, Bush, and Bush, the Tea Party should be doing all it can to ensure that Obamacare is a success – it plays right into their position as free enterprise advocates. It should be apparent that their candidates will need to explain themselves.

A Matter of Law

Let's consider what this might mean if it were a matter before the Supreme Court. We need not consider it as a matter for impeachment, because that would mean nobody raised the issue prior to nomination, or prior to the actual election.

Though, if both President and vice-President died in office, we might find it to be an issue caused by the line of succession. In the event that both were unable to fulfill the balance of their elected term, the order of succession would bring us to the Speaker of the House, then the President pro tempore of the Senate, and on to the Secretary of State, etc.

Given that a "natural born citizen" requirement doesn't apply to those who are elected to House or Senate, or occupy a "Secretarial" office, any one of these individuals could fail the Constitutional test, in which case, after whatever crisis brought about the transition has been resolved, impeachment might be in order.

For the sake of this examination, we will consider the following dozen possibilities which the court might consider in terms of the "natural born" wording, and the likely ruling. We are not dealing with the similar basis for citizenship under *The Immigration and Nationality Act* (INA).

1. Both parents are American Citizens and the birth occurred while parents are traveling abroad, and prior to a "due date" which would have seen the parents back in the States. POSSIBLE OK.

2. Both parents are American Citizens and born while mother is traveling abroad – this could include a day trip to Mexico or Canada; an extended trip to Europe or Asia. Again, a POSSIBLE OK. The fact that the child was premature should not serve to deny it of its birthright.

3. Both parents are American Citizens but they *intended* for the child to be born outside America and to have natural born status in another nation. NOT LIKELY.

4. Both parents are American Citizens but they renounced

their citizenship, or took citizenship in the foreign nation – than a definitive NO.

5. Both parents are American Citizens and birth was in American territory on foreign soil, or while one or both parents were in the service of the United States Government and therefore had to be out of the country. LIKELY YES. Parental service to the nation should not be held to be, or cited as, a reason to deprive a child of his natural birthright.

6. One parent is American but the child is born while both parents are in residence outside America – citizenship is statutory and derived, not Natural Born as meant in the Constitution.

7. The Mother is American and child is born to a foreign father, or prior to formal renunciation of his native citizenship, or pending his right to immigrate – citizenship is statutory and derived, not Natural Born as meant in the Constitution. (Had she wished child to be native born, or Natural Born as meant in the Constitution, mother could have returned to United States to have child; an exception could be made based on intend and premature birth, or third party interference with travel arrangements).

8. The Father is American and child is born to a foreign mother who is awaiting government permission to exit her country, or enter the United States – once again, the birth location being the result of third party interference, a case could be made for quasi-natural born status.

9. If the mother was kidnaped and transported to a foreign nation, or held against her will on foreign soil, the presumption is the child would have been born on American Soil and is therefore is NATURAL BORN.

10. The Court would hold that the term "Natural Born" means born on American soil, or in American sovereign territory, or while in the Service of the nation – or engaged in business & vacation related travels and birth is prior to original medically deduced "due date".

11. The Court would hold that the term "Statutory Citizenship" is a form of naturalization – an action involving a

general law enacted by Congress and signed by a President. The Court would also hold that this is different from a legal determination by the Congress that a specific set of circumstances constitutes "in service to the nation, or business & vacation travel."

12. A child who is born to missionaries, or individuals on extended business, or even a student engaged in foreign studies, could be granted Congressional sanction to meet the Natural Born test, providing none of the circumstances fit any of the previous possibilities, and there was never a stated intend, or formal act, by the mother to renounce her citizenship. Though it would be noted that the birth location was primarily one of free choice on the part of the parents.

We should also note that the American Congress has a presumptive obligation to clearly define, and enact into law, a debilitative definition of what constitutes "Natural Born." This is a clear mater of Constitutional integrity and therefore should take precedency over any discussions of the historic definition of marriage, or any application of a scientific definition of life as it might conflict with a biblical definition of birthright – the latter being attained when an individual, or any limb thereof, emerges from the womb.

However, should the Congress determine that "Natural Born" can be interpreted as a term for conception, then an individuals life, and all rights pertaining to citizenship, would begin at conception. Thus it could be held that anyone whose existence can be established to have begun with conception within the United States is a "Natural Born" American citizen.

As these possibilities apply to Ted Cruz, we have no idea where he was conceived, but we do know that his parents were working in Canada when he was born. We also know that his father was a Cuban national, and his mother a natural born American citizen and that he was, and has remained, a natural born citizen of Canada.

We know, from the 2008 Obama victory, that the Tea Party would demand a birth certificate from an individual whose passport records had clearly established he was born in Hawaii, almost two weeks shy of the second anniversary of Hawaiian Statehood.

But what if the parents were both American citizens by birth, and the child was born in abroad – how would the Republican Party respond?

Was Ted Cruz correct in his assertion to a Des Moines Register interviewer that every victorious Republican presidential candidate ran as a strong conservative?

If so, then he should stand at the forefront of a Conservative Constitutional interpretation of his own eligibility problem. We can reasonably hold that his level of intellectual honesty will determine if he allows himself to become a Presidential candidate.

Rather, it is entirely possible that the beginning of 2015 will have him raised to a position of either President, or President pro tem, of the United States Senate. That is, assuming a Republican electoral victory. Otherwise, he could easily become the next Senate Minority Leader, and remain a force in American politics for several decades and well into what is predicted to be the most tumultuous and important period in America and World history.

As of this writing, Americans consider al-Qaeda and other Islamic extremist groups to be their greatest threat, with 70% also ranking foreign cyber-attacks as a major threat – which places them on par with potential threats from Iran and North Korean's nuclear programs. As I will discus later, these risks, and finding solutions to the nations defective medical care system, are far more important than political attacks aimed at blocking potential solutions.

The question is, are there any leaders in America who can be seen to actually lead us to solutions, rather than obstruct those who are attempting to do so?

Of course, that isn't a secret. In December 2013, Obama made this challenge: "If Republicans have concrete plans that will actually reduce inequality, build the middle class, provide more ladders of opportunity to the poor, let's hear them. I want to know what they are. If you don't think we should raise the minimum wage, let's hear your idea to increase people's earnings. If you don't think every child should have access to preschool, tell us what you'd do differently to give them a better shot. If you still don't like Obamacare ... [laughter] ... even though it's built on market-based ideas of choice and competition in the private sector, then you should explain how, exactly, you'd cut costs, and cover more people, and make insurance more secure."

Recalling Tom Scully's role, we discover the trick that seems to have eluded that segment of the nation which has fun opposing everything Obama, or tagging everything his name. They did it when they renamed *The Affordable Care Act*. In an attempt to be somewhat derogatory, they re-christened it *Obamacare*. But the fact is, that single popular action had the effect of disavowing the input of, and origins with, the Republican leadership.

If you know that something is undeniably wrong – if you are discussing who should get the credit for a holocaust – then you may want to disavow. But if you have to fish around for things to assert and thus tarnish an idea that has yet to come into its own, you have a serious leadership problem.

Look at what Obama is doing with his challenge.

"Because I am their leader I must follow them." When I first heard the line, it was credited to the Marquis de Lafayette in a story which opens with him having a glass of wine in a Parisian café when someone burst in shouting, "Where is the mob going?" Lafayette gulped his remaining wine, pulled on his jacket and said "I don't know; but I have to get there first, because I am their leader!"

Obama is challenging those who would lead the mob to come up with ideas. And, as he did with Obamacare, he will race to the forefront – because he is their leader.

History is fickle. If Obamacare fails of its own volition, with no help from obstructionist, Obama will be blamed. If it succeeds, because the opposition renamed it for him, he will get the credit. If he runs to the front, he becomes the leader. If he is undermined, and the program is repealed, or there is a failed attempt to impeach him for political statements, history will reward him. Why is the Tea Party setting Obama up to be rewarded by history?

The 2013 Polling

Everyone with any interest in the character of the outcome of the 2016 election cycle began to make themselves known in December 2013. Operatives, donors, journalists and are speculating on who will run and on what platform. So far, we have all the usual suspects: Hillary Clinton, Chris Christie, Jeb Bush, Rand Paul, Ted Cruz, and Arnold Schwarzenegger.

Nobody is really going to debate Schwarzenegger, as he has no native born parent to extend a degree of validity to his campaign, and a Constitutional Amendment would achieve the very thing the Founding Fathers wanted to avoid – the possibility of any foreign agent, or nobility, asserting, or being granted, American leadership.

But, prior to the 2014 election – which will serve to define many aspects of both Federal and State political power structure – even known potential contenders are wary of the rush forward.

As chairman of the Republican Governor's Association, New Jersey Governor Chris Christie is a recognized power with national influence.

Christie has asserted, "I feel badly for President Obama. ... He just won a year ago, and everybody's like, 'So, who's next?' ... There is work to be done in this country. And as we shove him out the door, we minimize his ability to be an effective executive. And we shouldn't do that."

But it isn't just a question of shoving Obama "out the door," in reality, as we have seen, from the very start, there has been a concerted effort to undermine his presidency and the security of the American people.

Think about it. Just imagine why the Republicans, and the Tea Party, have offered absolutely no positive contributions to the solving of serious problems confronting those in the lower economic strata. Why the attack on Food Stamps? Why the attack on Health Care? Why the attack on Social Security? What possible agenda would justify their attack on the basic survival needs of upwards of a quarter of the American population?

Three years prior to the actual race, media organizations had already spent many thousands of dollars, and tens of thousands of man-hours, commissioning 2016 related polls.

One such poll is described by CNN Polling Director Keating Holland: "Among Republicans making more than $50,000, Christie wins 32% support, 20 points higher than Cruz, Ryan, or Marco Rubio, all of whom get 12% among higher-income GOPers, and 23 points higher than Paul. But among Republicans who make less than $50,000 a year, Christie's support drops 19 points, only good enough for second place behind Paul."

Ted Cruz, a freshman Republican Senator from Texas, has acquired a 2016 candidate status which is disproportional to his mere year or so of congressional experience; yet his actions are more closely scrutinized than any other of the Senatorial minority.

Why such attention to a man who is, without the slightest question, a *natural born* Canadian?

On the Democratic side, Hillary Rodham Clinton – former First Lady, former Secretary of State, with eight years experience as a United States Senator from New York – is routinely mentioned as a presidential contender. To these credentials, we can add that, candidate for the 2008 Democratic presidential nomination, Clinton won more primaries and delegates than any other female candidate in American history, and only narrowly lost to Obama.

On the Republican side, on 29 Nov 2013, The Christian Post published an article by Star Parker in which she described the ideal 2016 Republican 'Dream Team' – Senator Ted Cruz and Dr. Ben Carson. A team which Parker declared would immediately bring forth unanimous agreement between Democrats and establishment Republicans: " I hope Star is right. This will guarantee another four years of our big government socialism. These Tea Party whackos could never win."

But Parker made the point that "that leaders ...don't start by asking people what they want and trying to give it to them. [They] see what the problems are that need to be solved and they deliver solutions that customers are not aware of or never dreamed of."

Parker goes on to dismiss polling as yesterday's news, and points to several points she deems relevant:

1. The ongoing dismal performance of American economy;
2. An ongoing dismal breakdown of the American family.
3. The deep dissatisfaction with the state of the country;
4. The direction the nation is moving; and
5. A uniformly low trust in government and political leaders.

given the sweeping demographic changes of the country, it can't hurt to hear this from two self-made Americans – one of Spanish-speaking roots (Cruz's father immigrated from Castro's Cuba) and one African American raised in a ghetto in Detroit.

According to Parker, a Cruz-Carson ticket would provide voters with a clear, no-nonsense and honest alternative to the two established party agendas. She characterizes the two men as being Americans committed to "what America is about and what made it great." Things which she summarizes as limited government, free markets, and traditional values, accompanied by a strong national allegiance devoid of interest in political game playing.

Parker then goes on to mention that, in light of the sweeping demographic changes in America, the that these are two self-made men – one, via his father's Cuban origin, Hispanic, and the other an African American from the Detroit ghetto who became a pioneering neurosurgeon credited with the first successful separation of twin conjoined at the head.

Supposedly, both men hold that personal success is not about government programs, rather it is derived from taking personal responsibility for one's life in an environment where freedom is not about claiming and taking, but rather is derived from about creating and serving. But this serving apparently begins with a Canadian's right to ignore, or claim exemption from, Constitutional restriction

A month before the Parker article, political commentator and television host, Bill Maher appeared on, *Piers Morgan Live* , to state he believes that, in a head to head competition, Senator Ted Cruz would beat Republican New Jersey Governor Chris Christie for the 2016 presidential nomination.

Maher made the point that people should not underestimate Cruz, who has become an hero to the conservative base because he has lived up to his campaign promise and stuck it to the Republican establishment during the battle to defund Obamacare.

Maher stated, "He is definitely going to be the favorite of the people who vote in Republican primaries. I mean, we saw what it looked like the last time and the time before ... But the problem with the Republican primaries last time for them, they said they didn't have a Ted Cruz in there. That's why they went with Mitt Romney. Remember, they tried every other person, every other Republican got a shot at being number one..." Concluding, "You know, if it's the primary voters who vote every time, I think it will be Ted Cruz."

Maher's logic included the fact that Gov. Christie is from the Northeast, and has "put his arm around" President Barack Obama after Hurricane Sandy. To that we can add the Christie was quick to latch on to his state's share of the new Obamacare funding – so Christie is not about to defund Obamacare and thereby destroy his claim to a New Jersey, and Northeast, voter base.

Another poll has revealed that, despite shutting down the government, costing the nation $24 billion, and the associated debt ceiling debate crisis, Ted Cruz hasn't lost any ground with support among Republican voters in Texas. The left-leaning Public Policy Polling (PPP), discovered 32 percent of Texas Republican voters wanted Cruz as their presidential candidate in 2016.

The Raleigh, North Carolina based polling firm also revealed that Florida Gov. Jeb Bush polled only 13 percent; New Jersey Gov. Chris Christie, 10 percent; tied at 6 percent were Kentucky Sen. Rand Paul and Louisiana Gov. Bobby Jindal; with Florida Sen. Marco Rubio and Wisconsin Rep. Paul Ryan coming in with only 5 percent. Of interest is the fact that 2012 candidates, Gov. Rick Perry of Texas and former Pennsylvania Sen. Rick Santorum had received a mere 3 percent among Texas Republican voters.

Though Cruz actually gained 7 points over a similar poll ruin prior to the shutdown, fully half of the Texans polled believe he has been bad for the state's reputation. And, in terms of a run against

Hillary Clinton, Gov. Jeb Bush appears to be viewed as the strongest competition, while Gov. Rick Perry is seen as a "don't even bother to run" candidate.

When we look to the nationals, Chris Christie could garner 24 percent of Republicans and independents, which is seven-points above an earlier CNN poll, a rise that might reflect the fact he was re-elected to a second term as New Jersey Governor in a landslide.

According to the same poll: Sen. Ted Cruz of Texas drew only 10 percent; Sen. Marco Rubio of Florida, 9 percent; Texas Gov. Rick Perry, 7 percent; that left former Florida Gov. Jeb Bush and former Sen. Rick Santorum of Pennsylvania tied at 6 percent.

Thus far, the same CNN poll showed Hillary Clinton carrying 63 percent of Democrats and independents.

We also need to consider that these polls wer taken at a time when an ABC News/Washington Post poll, showed 55 percent of Americans disapproved of the job Obama was doing, and that, in an election redux, former Massachusetts Governor Mitt Romney would have ousted Obama.

However, this early in the process, polls reflect individuals for whom the respondents register name recognition , and it is rare that anyone would claim they'd vote for someone they have never heard of. Most of the names bandied about belong to politicians who do not have neither national reputation, nor name recognition.

More importantly, because they are years away from critical campaigning, the mud has yet to be slung and issues like those of the 'Birthists' have yet to emerge as a real factor in the process.

What do we know of Birthism and Birthists? Are they for real, or just racists in disguise?

As Senator Ted Cruz moves into the nomination process, will the Birthists remain quiet, or will they denounce him as ineligible?

Maybe they will work tirelessly to undermine his competition – remaining noticeable quiet about where he was born as they have been. If they do, they will set the stage for a Democratic victory, or a clear Constitutional Crisis which will paralyze American power.

Birthism and Birther

The terms Birthist and Birthism can be seen as related terms utilized in two distinct, but politically related, contexts.

Under one heading, these terms can be related to 'Right-to-Life' anti-abortionist elements, or those who demand documented proof citizenship by birth – an actual birth certificate.

In terms of definition, a google search resulted in a Birthist being defined as "those who believes in aborting the rights of others on the basis of whether or not they have been born, often to the point of justifying their deliberate destruction."

Thus google yielded a definition which would relate to the rights which could be accorded a fetus. Essentially, those rights being no different than the Biblical definition of a 'birthright,' or the right bestowed upon a child as soon as any part of its body emerges from the womb as established in the story of Jacob and his brother first-to-emerge twin brother Esau (Genesis 25).

As defined by the story, the first twin to stick out a limb is deemed the first born, and thus entitled to all the rights accorded a first born son, Esau; it did not matter that his brother, Jacob, was the first child to wholly emerge. Thus, in biblical terms, there are no rights accorded until some portion of the child emerges.

In terms of personhood – as defined in the context of murder – the matter is somewhat different. In Exodus 21, we find that any attack on a pregnant woman, which results in her losing the child, is deemed murder. Thus, in terms of abortion – which is done with express permission of the woman – there is no act of violence, no attack as defined in that or other biblical laws; therefore there is no prohibition against abortion, or act of murder.

Exodus 21:22 is explicit, the death of the fetus is not murder, rather it is an action requiring monetary compensation from those who caused the miscarriage. There is no explicit religious basis to oppose abortion, but ignoring 21:22 would be spiritually punishable under St. Paul's mandate – if you are on of his Gentiles (Christian).

Even within the context of 'murder', the crime is not in a loss of life, but in the loss of an heir without the consent of the parents. With parental consent, the consent of the mother, by an intentional medical act, there is no scriptural basis to assert the taking of a life.

In terms of this 'Birthist' definition, if one declares a fetus to have a birthright, then one would also have to grant it all rights and privileges which would otherwise exist upon its emerging from the womb. Thus, if we were to define human life as beginning with conception, then all, and full, rights of citizenship would also begin, or be denied, at the time of conception.

A child conceived in the United States would be 'a natural born American' – without having actually been born. Similarly, a child conceived outside the border of the United States, might well be entitled to citizenship via its parent, or parents, but it would NOT legally be entitled to the status of 'a natural born American'.

Of course, the problem becomes one of determining where and when a fetus was conceived. Moreover, where paternity is concerned, absent any test of the child's DNA, the father's place of origin could not be utilized to establish nationality. It's a matter of the old West Indian expression *"Mama Know, Father Maybe."*

Hareidi Jews, known collectively as the Hareidim, are an ultra-orthodox branch of the Hebrew faith who assert that a child is Jewish, if its mother is Jewish.

As I have pointed out in several books associated with Jewish knowledge and historical origins of tradition, the Hareidim, or the European Hasidim, disregard the biblical paternal lineage structure to assert a *"Mama Know, Father Maybe"* logic which infers a need to raise questions about their own Jewish origins – which is a DNA problem they will need to content with on both their X & Y lines.

Historically, ancient societies were matrilineal, everything passed through the female line – this changed with *'Genesis.'*

But, we are seeking to view the matter in terms of how they have been viewed by those who have asserted Barack Obama was not 'a natural born American' and therefore is not Constitutionally eligible to be President, and are confronted by the absolute certainty that Ted Cruz was born in Canada, and yet he polls as a frontrunner for the Republican presidential nomination.

It is that definition of 'Birther,' one who would attack Ted.

Of course, the election in 2014, and that of 2016, will rest on the perception of dishonesty and hypocrisy among those who back each candidate – as well as the emergence of those characteristics in the candidate themself.

Each party carries, or provides, the brush with which it can eventually be tarred. If is a matter of reciprocity – the Golden Rule with which Rafael Cruz, Ted's father, should be intimately familiar, so I'll look at Rafael in the next chapter. For now, we will simply note that, on the Senatorial campaign trail, father and son were always together, and Rafael Cruz was always in the wings, standing in the shadows as his son walked out into the spotlight which eventually followed him onto the Senate floor.

Under the rules of reciprocity – which certainly would apply to an Evangelical Minister and his politician son – we expect to be treated the way we treat others, and those we deal with have every reason to believe they will be treated the way they treat us. If, by being dishonest or hypocritical, they show us disrespect and that they cannot be trusted, they have no reason to expect our support – and certainly we would not want them, or the people promoted by them, to represent our interests.

When we look at Birther assertions about Obama, it is self-evident that, they honestly believe their assertions, we would see them level the same, or similar, charges against any for whom there is clear evidence that the charges are warranted.

The elephant in the room is not the theories about Obama's birth. There was a timely birth announcement published, and that publication was based on a list of births provided by the hospital to the Department of Health, which then recorded the data and, in a routine manner, provided it to the Honolulu newspapers.

If Obama had been born outside the nation, his mother's passport record would establish that – as every genealogist knows, immigration records are very specific; everyone who legally enters any nation is recorded. Thus, had he been born outside America, there would be a record of the mother and baby entering America.

Obama's school records would also show his place of birth. If they were falsified, the deceit would not be his, but his mother's. But even more significant than his mothers travel documents would be his father's. They would have traveled to a Third World country for his mother given birth in Kenya – traveled there with his father – which means, because his father was an alien, that there would be far more immigration documents (in Kenya and America).

Then there is the fact that Obama's father went to Harvard Law on a scholarship. To go to law school requires all the usual applications, and the taking of a test – LSAT – for which he would have had to have been in the States. So now we find the window of opportunity to travel narrows significantly.

Had Obama been born just two years and a month earlier, prior to Hawaii being a state, the Birthers would have had a case.

Beginning in 1961, various Public officials would have to have falsified the data provided the newspaper, as well as that which was officially filled. Immigration records would have had to be falsified. And to what end? As the child of an American citizen mother, the infant Obama was as legally an American citizen as the infant Ted Cruz would be he entered the country five years after his birth.

Reciprocity – the Birther movement is designed to treat the average American as if they are total idiots. They believe the have a meaningful constituency among people who are clearly considered too stupid to think.

Why would all those agencies, in 1961, falsify sequentially compiled records, lists of who was on what plane, or ship, or born in what hospital, with all the other people were also recorded. Why would the names of Obama, his mother and father be omitted from the immigration record, and his name added to the Health Department birth record and newspaper announcement in 1961?

Fortunately, just because a Birther movement is part of the Obama opposition, it does not mean it is representative of the Tea Party – unless the Tea Party members are repeating the exact same conspiracy theories. But, would they blatantly lie to the public?

Rafael Cruz

To judge the son, look to the father. We might not hold that the sins of the father should be vested on the sons, but we do know that parents and their children display similar traits and beliefs. We can also say, with some degree of assurance, to the extent that sons tend to follow in their father's footsteps, and to do much of the things their fathers did before them, fathers and sons resemble each other. In recent years we saw this with President Bush Senior and Junior – and might well see it again if Jeb Bush were to become President – both of whom increased the National Debt and engaged in a war with Iraq.

Reportedly, when giving a dominionist sermon, at the New Beginnings Church in Irving, Texas, on August 26, 2012, Rafael Cruz called for "kings" such as his son Ted to rule America, and then take money from all non-evangelical Christians and redistribute it to fundamentalists – both clergy and parishioners.

The Pastor of the Church, Larry Huch, drew upon Proverbs 13:22 in support of the idea which Cruz then phrased as "the wealth of the wicked is stored for the righteous. And it is through the kings, anointed to take dominion, that that transfer of wealth is going to occur."

In part, we know Pastor Huch said, "I know that's why God got Rafael's son elected – Ted Cruz, the next Senator. But here's the exciting thing – and that's why I know it's timely for him to teach this, and bring this anointing. This will begin what we call the 'End Time Transfer of Wealth.' ... And that when these gentiles begin to receive this blessing, they will never go back financially through the valley again. God is looking at the church, and everyone in it, and deciding, in the next 3 and 1/2 years, who will be his bankers. And the ones that say, 'Here am I, Lord, you can trust me', we will become so blessed that we will usher in the coming of the Messiah."

Huch even invoked dominionist numerology to assert that, "The number 12 means 'divine government', that God begins to rule and reign. Not Wall Street, not Washington - God's people and his kingdom will begin to rule and reign."

Granted, having written several books on the Bible over the past thirty-odd years, I'm no stranger to the meaning behind the numbers, or to asserting that they indicate some wicked-bad times will occur between 2034/5 and 2064/5, but nothing supports the assertions made by Huch and Cruz Sr.

That said, I would note that, before introducing Rafael Cruz to his congregation, Huch, at the dawn of 2012, made the assertion – that is apparently supported by divine words – which draws our focus to the 'divine' importance of the election period of 2015/16.

In his sermon, Pastor Cruz then asserted, "There are some of you, as a matter of fact I will dare to say the majority of you, that your anointing is not an anointing as priest. It's an anointing as king. And God has given you an anointing to go to the battlefield. And what's the battlefield? The battlefield is the marketplace. To go to the marketplace and occupy the land ... and take dominion.

"If you remember the last time I was in this pulpit, I talked to you about Genesis chapter 1, verse 28, where God says unto Adam and Eve, 'Go forth, multiply, TAKE DOMINION over all creation.' And if you recall, we talked about the fact that that dominion is not just in the church. That dominion is over every area – society, education, government, economics ...”

Is Ted Cruz on a divine mission to confiscate (in the Lord's name) the wealth of society? Does Cruz hold the same convictions as his father and believe that he is to be a *'king, anointed to take dominion'*, or a divine servant of a Messiah who will emerge after, maybe in time for, the 2016 election?

In terms of a socialist agenda, we have Cruz Sr. Calling for a divinely commanded "redistribution of wealth" from the wealthy to the needy – but with the proviso those needy are also Evangelical Christians. Moreover, his will be a greater "transfer of wealth" then simple broad-based Entitlements or Welfare; when it comes to the simple things like Social Security, Medicaid, Medicare, or 'God Forbid" Obamacare, you better belong to his church.

Of course, when I saw the following words, which invoke

rabbinical teaching, I could not help but think of my 2012 book, **Saint Paul's Joke**, "But here's the exciting thing... The rabbinical teaching is... that in a few weeks begins that year 2012 and that this will begin what we call the end-time transfer of wealth. And that when these Gentiles begin to receive this blessing, they will never go back financially through the valley again.'"

Saint Paul was very specific about the rules his Gentiles had to follow – they had to be '*kosher*'; they had to follow all 613 of the Hebrew laws, and if they had children, than those children – by law – would have had to be circumcised.

I wonder if Ted Cruz is circumcised, because Peter and Jesus would certainly not have recognized someone [as being among the anointed] who wasn't. And, for that matter, if they didn't follow ALL the laws, they didn't even have the authority to criticize a Jew who ignored those laws – or so said Paul.

The invocation of religion has interesting ramifications. It can be used as a basis to attack, or defend. It serves as a basis for genocide – as it has for thousands of years – or as the basis for all that we deem ethical and proper when treating others as we would have them treat us.

What did Ted Cruz learn at his father's feet? And how will that affect the reality of a President Cruz?

Talking in Hood County, Texas on April 25, 2013, Pastor Cruz asserted of the Obama Administration: "The government is going to take all of your money and Obama has no problem with murder." Which, if you think about it, in light of his 2012 sermon, is rather interesting – he is saying Obama is doing exactly what 'the anointed' will be doing after the 2016 election.

Cruz is also on record as labeling any attempt by Obama to take executive action against Climate Change to be an example of tyranny. It appears, the father is against efforts to stem global warming and protect America's coastal cities, and their populations, from flooding and the type of catastrophic storms which we have begun to see reeking havoc around the world.

In terms of Climate Change, we need to note that is a product of burning inefficient fossil fuels; the least efficient being wood or coal, then oil, and finally the most efficient, natural gas. So we have a valid question: How would President Ted Cruz, or any candidate elected with Tea Party approval, address Climate Change?

In reality, currently America's biggest supplier of oil appears to be his son's place of birth, Canada, and where Cruz Sr. And his wife owned a seismic-data processing firm for Canadian oil drillers. But Cruz is correct when he states that our enemies have the power "to shut down the valves and bring us to our knees." We saw that during the Carter era oil embargo, and we will see it again when we have depleted our reserves and are fully dependent on foreign oil.

But creating that dependence has been a Republican policy, ever since Ronald Reagan tore the solar collectors from the White House roof and initiated the denunciation of Climate Change or the need for sustainable energy as a matter of National Security.

At the Family Leadership Summit in Ames, Iowa, Pastor Cruz denounced gay marriage as some form of government conspiracy, saying, "Socialism requires that government becomes your god. That's why they have to destroy the concept of God. They have to destroy all loyalties except loyalty to the government. That's what's behind homosexual marriage. It's really more about the destruction of the traditional family than about exalting homosexuality, because you need to destroy, also, loyalty to the family."

Curiously, it is Russia, the gestation place of Marxist socialist thought, which is at the forefront of the renewed attacks on LGBT rights – which places Cruz and Socialist Russia on the same team.

At least now we know why Sen. Mitch McConnell (R-Ky) has denounced the Tea Party Republicans as "giving conservatism a bad name" and "participating in ruining the [Republican] brand."

McConnell has gone on to say, "To have the kind of year we ought to have in 2014, we have to have electable candidates on November ballots in every state — people that don't scare the general electorate and can actually win, because winners make policy and losers go home. We can't just turn the other cheek and hope for the best. It didn't work in 2010 and 2012 so we're going to try something different in 2014."

The question then arises, if Cruz is speaking to the Tea Party choir, and McConnell is address the rest of the Republican Party, how are the two going to become sufficiently unified [by November 2014] to hope to field a successful presidential candidate for 2016? Is 'The Lord' going to step in and raise up someone and, contrary to the mandates of St. Paul, deny marriage which is mandated as the basis for having anything which does not constitute a Paul's celibate lifestyle?

But there is an element of reciprocity contained in the idea that we can judge the son, by looking at the father. We can assess the fathers, by looking at the sons. We know that both Ted Cruz and Barack Obama are brilliant – the fact that they graduated *magna cum laude* from Harvard Law School establishes that – so we can reasonably assert their father's intelligence. We know that Cruz Sr. operated his own computer based seismic analysis firm; we also know that Obama Sr. attended Harvard Law on a scholarship; that is sufficient to infer and assert paternal intelligence.

Therefore, if an obviously intelligent man makes what seem to be ignorant, or blatantly stupid, remarks, we need to look at those remarks a bit closer. This is especially true when the speaker is a man accustomed to preaching a religion that is rich in parables and has routinely concealed information in code.

Rafael Bienvenido Cruz is now an Evangelical Minister, and as I established in my 2012 book, *Genesis of Genesis* – where, for the first time since the destruction of the Second temple, two thousand years ago, the secret of the Patriarch ages was revealed – the Torah, or Pentateuch (the first five books of the Old Testament), could, in a secular context, be considered an encyclopedia of legal, medical, astronomical and historical knowledge concisely encoded and credited to the source of all Wisdom and Knowledge. With the New Testament, we had the promise that their would come a time of Understanding that would accompany a judgement period. It is a reality to which Rafael Cruz has dedicated his life – so what is he really saying?

At a North Texas Tea Party Meeting on September 12, 2012, Rafael Cruz is said to have proclaimed that "Marxist Obama should go 'back to Kenya.'" A statement which clearly ignores the reality of Barack Obama – both the established fact that he was born in the State of Hawaii, and that even his Affordable Care Act is not a single payer socialist program, but rather it is a private sector controlled program originally proposed by Republican Conservative President Ronald Reagan, and then again redrawn in basically its current form by Republican President George W. Bush.

There is a quote associated with an apparent talk before the Tyler, Texas based organization, *Grassroots America We the People* (GAWTP), in October 2012, in which Cruz Sr. Allegedly says, "the oil industry is stifled [by Obama regulations] ... We are buying 40 percent of our oil from our enemies ... Our enemies control the energy that we use or do not use ... to shut down the valves and bring us to our knees."

America does rely on foreign sources for about 45 percent of its oil, but about half of that from the Western Hemisphere, and the largest supplier is our ally, Canada, which also has seven times the proven oil reserves of the USA. As for the other nations, many are unreliable. To that we can add that policies established by Ronald Reagan have left America quickly depleting its own reserves without ever having initiated the type of alternative energy solutions which have been adopted in Northern Europe.

When he asserts that "our enemies control the energy that we use or do not use," Rafael Cruz is correct. But, in the context of his 'anointed' speech, he is pointing to the future – a future which will come to pass during the next presidential term, the term of office for the individual who will be elected in 2016.

Cruz's homeland, Cuba, reportedly has total reserves of about 20 billion barrels of liquid crude, mostly in offshore oil fields. Due to the longstanding United States embargo against Cuba, no U.S. companies are participating in their development or recovery.

By contrast, the USA has proven oil reserves of 26.5 billion barrels, and a reserves-to-production ratio averaging 11.26 years in

2007; the recession then created a situation where, in 2008-9, the USA became a net exporter of refined products, thereby distorting the domestic ratio.

Effectively the Bush recession, following upon Republican approved outsourcing policies, created a situation where America depleted its reserves in order to maintain its balance of payments.

In contrast to America, Iraq's reserve-to-production ratio is estimated at 158 years; the he crude and condensate ratio for the top 20 international oil producing companies is 73 years, but actual established global reserves will only last into the year 2050-2055.

Obviously we could continue to review the various statistics, but it would appear that, by the end of the presidential term which begins in January 2017, the America will have difficulty producing enough domestic oil to support our military, much less our SUV's and fossil fuel supported lifestyle – and that is the issue Rafael Cruz was addressing.

A policy based upon a uniform and systemic denial of facts is precisely what is necessary to ensure apocalyptic outcomes. If, in 2020, America is totally dependent on foreign oil, it is also totally removed from providing any meaningful foreign military presence.

As an Evangelical Minister, Rafael Cruz would be familiar with Matthew 23:13-29, where Jesus denounces hypocrisy. Thus, when he talks of a "Marxist", who should return to the nation of his father [for Obama, Kenya; for Ted, Cuba] he might well have been speaking in terms of a parable. Consider the Castro family in Cuba. Fidel Castro has been a defacto 'king' since the revolution, and he recently pass the crown to his brother, Raúl Castro, as his successor.

Development of the Cuban oil reserves is currently in the hands of foreign leaseholders, none of who are clearly friends of the Cuban Communists. Could Cruz's speeches be encoding a message to the Cuban people, one in which his son becomes their 'anointed king'? If not, then Rafael has serious problems with honesty and rationality – problems which are contaminating the Republican party and threaten its destruction. On the other hand, destruction of the Republican Party might be the ultimate Tea Party objective.

The Issues 1

In promoting prophecies of some divinely inspired wealth redistribution, Cruz Sr must deal with reality of the global economy.

For years, American businesses has sought to have Congress address the problem caused by special-interest tax breaks, which has necessitated a 35 percent tax on corporate profits – making the tax on American business the highest in the developed world.

Were special interest tax rates – jointly promoted by the Tea Party and Conservative Republicans – eliminated, the rate on corporate income could be reduced, and American business would become more competitive in the global economy.

Clearly, if it is not resolved by a change in Congress in 2014, this is an issue for the 2016 election.

But Rafael Cruz has educated his son to believe that socialist redistribution of wealth is the inevitable outcome of events leading up to, and thereafter following from, the 2016 election.

The 2013 winter recess saw the Senate Finance Committee drafting a proposal which would end the practice of indefinitely deferring U.S. taxes on foreign earnings. The same draft document would have an immediate 20 percent tax imposed on roughly $2 trillion in profits being sequestered in overseas corporate accounts; it would also sharply curtail immediate deduction for expenses, such as advertising, which should properly be associated with any revenues generated. Thus, brand recognition or image advertising would be treated as a depreciable asset, rather than an immediate time of expenditure expense.

In may regards, after decades of talk, Congress has as yet never dealt with the reality of the famed "Three Martini Lunch" – it isn't a "lunch" it is a class of executive perk at taxpayer expense, which serves no real business purpose.

In an idea business environment, all taxes would be conform to the structure originally envisioned by the Founding Fathers – a flat rate on real earnings, with the possibility of a deduction to cover the value of productive expenditures.

In the original Constitution, prior to the 1913 Amendment, labor could keep what it earned. Of course, the nature of labor and the production of wealth has changed to a point where that is no longer a feasible option. Yep it would be practical for America to adopt a variation on the Rafael Cruz 'divine distribution' approach.

America could allow personal deductions to be set in accord with the prevailing poverty rate, and make a refundable deduction – one which would have every family file a tax return and receive a payment for the funds needed to bring them up to the designated poverty level. This would require that the Supplemental Nutrition Assistance Program (SNAP, or Food Stamps) and other programs be counted as income for filing purposes.

The net effect would be to reduce welfare costs and suppress welfare fraud – each recipient would need to file a corresponding tax form, complete with a valid Social Security Number.

Illegal immigrants might have significant difficulty collecting any funds or extended governmental benefits.

In that regard, we also have the issue of the "welfare Kings and Queens" – very dramatic, but rhetoric which ignores the reality of full-time workers, and retirees, who aren't paid sufficiently well as to be disqualified from public assistance. In point of fact, some employers utilize public assistance as part of their business model; and Social Security utilizes other governmental to underwrite their below survival rate payment scale. Thus, what is being 'saved' via the low Social Security payments is actually being paid out through, and subsidized by, a more complex and costly series of entitlement programs designed to raise people to poverty level.

But that is an issue, or proposal, which is unlikely to emerge in a campaign. It is far easier to bemoan the possible existence of something that to risk the reality of showing it exists and addressing the problem. It is always easier to be against an issue, than to offer any solution – a fact which is evident from the Tea Party approach to Obamacare.

One clear issue for 2016 will be the ability of a candidate to offer clear solutions to perceived problems – especially those which they raise as valid campaign issues. Rafael Cruz does appear to be correct in pointing to 2016 as a watershed period in history, and for that we will need answers, not empty, generally negative, rhetoric of the type which seems to have marked the anti-Obama debate.

Among the issues associated with the possibility of the first overhaul of the tax code since 1986 would be the fact Republican leaders asked Ways and Means Committee Chairman Dave Camp (R-Mich.) to withhold any proposal which might distract attention from the botched rollout of Obama's health-care law. Thus the pre-election 2014 agenda is controlled by a deliberate attempt to do a disservice to the American people.

Thus, the issues for 2014, become those which distract from serving the rightful issues related to the public's business. There is a reality, if they are quiet about the problems with Obamacare, the ability to utilize the failures in the final days of a campaign will be enhanced. They could rightly say "we gave it every chance, but it is clearly apparent '*they*' are not up to the task."

Instead, but being obvious in their obstructionist approach, the Republicans open themselves to be labeled as the cause of the failures: "If not for their persistent obstructionist policies, and their consistent blocking of corrective measures, the program would be working." Or, assuming the bugs are worked out, the argument becomes: "Despite their persistent obstructionism and disregard for the real business before them, we have achieved ..."

Curiously, distracting attention from the botched rollout of Obama's health-care law would serve them better in the days just before voters actually go to the polls. This would be especially true if they could point to some solid achievements which could be utilized to justify that they could achieve so much more if they had better representation in the House and Senate.

Think about this. At the close of 2013, with only six months in which to define the issues which will define the 2014 election, and set the stage for their candidate to ride to victory in 2016, the Republicans have chosen to run against the efficiency of a piece of troubled software. Moreover, it is software which is, in essence, simply duplicating programs that can be found in any state which was willing to accept Obamacare Medicaid funds.

On December first, two months after its initial launch, the government website appeared to be functioning according to design. At that point, the Republicans began raising security claims and inferring there was a vulnerability which hackers might use. As has been their standard policy, they ignored the firewall upgrades and provided no evidence of vulnerabilities.

On December first, it was reported that the site's average response time was under one second, down from eight seconds in October, and, allowing for ongoing maintenance, will be functional 95 percent of the time. While the site was not as yet ready to handle peak anticipated loads, it was reportedly able to process 800,000 users per day, and 50,000 users at a single time.

If we look to Gov. Chris Christie's basic approach, one which simply accepted Obamacare as the law of the land, the net result was to help needy low-income people, make hospitals more stable, and save the State of New Jersey a respectable amount of money – an estimated $227 million in the first year alone.

In real terms – those which are the basis for voter decisions – the rejection of Obamacare money becomes an issue if Medicaid expansion becomes a drag on the state budget. Irregardless of whether or not the state accepted the funds, the various expansion policies will go into effect; voters might find themselves deprived of services available in neighboring states, or taxpayers will be faced with compensating for any shortfalls.

Abstract ideological nonsense might justify battles in the political areas, but in the real world of the ballot box, average voters want their lives improved – or, at the very least, as good, or better than that of their neighbors in adjoining states.

In reality, Christie's decision meant 300,000 low-income New Jerseyans will receive health coverage, and, over the next decade, the state will receive over $15 billion in federal Medicaid funds. Which raises the questions of how many billions of dollars were lost by to states whose 'conservative' Governors chose to deny their residents both the federal funds and expanded Medicaid.

One issue to be dealt with in 2014, will be the fact that fifty-million voters will be age sixty-five or older. Will this group might vote their ideology, it is more likely that they will vote their wallets and the projected welfare of their grandchildren.

Offsetting this is the fact, the demographic which has always supported insurance, the '*invincibles*', were basically unaware of a requirement that they buy healthcare policies. With a third of the primary market unaware Obamacare – even after the shutdown – one needs to wonder how they address the actual issues which will affect their future and the success of a private-sector program.

In 2014, the number of U.S. workers should approach 162.1 million people, or roughly 15 million more than the labor force a decade earlier. In addition, as of 2013, 90.5 million Americas don't work and are not counted as part of the labor force – a sizable proportion of that number comprise those some politicians refer to as voters who are too lazy to work.

Given the 2007-2009 recession, efforts to deprive people of the standard of living they probably remember having as children ... well, not all that politically bright. For that reason it could be anticipated that the strongest 'conservative' base would be those who, historically, experienced the lowest standard of living; or had the lowest family educational background.

Clearly birth control and abortion will remain issues. But we must recall that, in terms of religion, children didn't belong to the women, they were God's and not really hers. But, as we know from scripture, God declared personhood exists only at birth.

In the church dominated middle ages, unwanted babies were left by the thousands at Church-run hospitals and foundling homes, only to be killed by the nuns and priests. We now know that death rates at foundling homes were as high as 90 percent. But, as long as it was men making that decision, it was totally acceptable.

If you consider modern 'Right-to-Life' logic, it is still the men who dictate when a woman should have a child, and it is those same men who, in the various legislatures, deny her and the children they mandate to be born, any ongoing support. It is a matter of basic Conservative policy. Deny healthcare, cut educational funds, and promote any militaristic activity which seems in vogue – under no circumstances however will you provide support for the child you mandate be born because a condom malfunctioned, or the woman raped.

We must also note that, until the Supreme Court stepped in, it was considered acceptable to murder the woman – by denying an abortion – when he fetus was not only not viable, but would either kill her or render her sterile. Thus, even a if woman wanted that child, and would quickly replace one lost due to life-threatening medical complications, the 'Right-to-Life' sponsors advocated she die or end up with complications resulting in her sterilization. And, when pressed on the point, they still advocate for the death or the sterilization of the mother due to birth abnormalities which would be best addressed immediate abortion – regardless of trimester.

Still it could be argued that a woman's lot – at least in western nations – is considerably better now then it was during the Victorian and Edwardian era. In that period, conservative men, who were doctors – a profession women were barred from entering – refused women any form of anesthesia. The justification was the same then as now, and derived from a paternalistic interpretation of scripture: Genesis 3:16 – "I will surely multiply your pain in childbearing; in pain you shall bring forth children. Your desire shall be for your husband, and he shall rule over you."

In that one verse, the Egyptian matrilineal system was ended, and the natural pain associated with 'out-of-water' birthing, became the law of western civilization. But its adoption also caused **Saint Paul's Joke**, in which we learn that the acceptance of any part of the Old Testament Law mandates acceptance of ALL the laws – or the individual, according to Paul, will be among those who Jesus stated He would not know. But that is more in keeping with things Rafael Cruz would have to deal with among his congregation.

Cruz claims to be a 'Born Again Christian' Evangelical. This infers that he is a Christian via St. Paul, who brought in the Gentiles – and required very specific things of them. Unfortunately, there is nothing about Cruz Sr, or Jr, which would assert that they are, indeed following the teachings, or doctrinal mandates, of Paul, and raises serious questions as to their objectives and true allegiances.

If we think in terms of the October Shutdown, if you are old enough, you might imagine the reality behind: "Nothing is any more obnoxious than good ideas from those you oppose."

H.G. Wells, said "Moral indignation is jealousy with a halo."

There is a lot of moral indignation in Congress – sufficient to justify closing the government for sixteen days, thereby costing the American economy $24 Billion, and threatening the destruction of the 'Full faith and Credit" of the American monetary system. WHY?

Tom, liked the market-driven private-insurance exchanges, but, while not opposed to the programs, or the law, he just fears that rapid transfer of hundreds of billions of dollars in future subsidies – designed to help families earning up to $95,000 buy insurance – might divert funds from other parts of the economy. If so, that could have an overall negative effect. "It's way too much money, way too fast," he said. "But it's going to be great for you investors."

Thus we have a Conservative Republican declare Obamacare is "great for investors" – which means great fro free enterprise and the Republican economic base. So why would the Tea Party attack a program which is ideal for it's own political parent party? Could it be the sin of envy – that a Democratic President managed to do what three Republican Presidents before him couldn't … enact a Republican program designed to enhance the private sector?

Or could it be that the Tea Party base are no different than Moses' sister, Miriam – who we know was punished by HaShem for attacking the wife of Moses because she was Ethiopian (Black).

If the Tea Party is willing to destroy the American economy, and threaten to undermine the global economy – just because they attempted 42 times in one year to repeal, or defund, Obamacare and failed – what other extremes will they go to, if they don't get their own way on other Republican initiatives?

Is the American economy their true target, or enemy?

The Issues 2

Al Qaeda remains a viable obstacle to peace in the world, and cross-referencing the words of Rafael Cruz with the final chapters of **Saint Paul's Joke** and we have template, or roadmap, for the real problems which will confront whoever is a candidate in 2016, and then the President in 2017.

In the beginning of December 2013, an Islamist group linked to al Qaeda had taken root in the occupied Palestinian territory. It is already established that they have an Iraqi presence, but having destabilized the region with the 12-year American 'War on Terror', Israel and Saudi Arabia have become critical to any restoration of stability in the region.

A *Holy Warriors' Assembly* (Majles Shura al-Mujahideen), statement posted on an Islamist web forum announced their presence with the words: "By the will of God Almighty, the global jihadi doctrine has reached the bank of pride, the West Bank, planting its foothold after all attempts to thwart its presence."

This group is a clear and present danger to efforts by both the Palestinian Authority and Israel to establish a peaceful region along their joint border, the associated negotiations which, it is believed, which could lead to West Bank Palestinian statehood.

Majles Shura al-Mujahideen denounced those peacemaking efforts and threatened attacks on both the Palestinian Authority and Israel, asserting: "We call on every sincere person to cut off what is called 'negotiations', which cause one's nose to turn away with its foul stench of collaboration. We are serious about fighting the aggression against religion by the blaspheming Jews and the hypocritical collaborators."

Since the start of the Syrian civil war in March 2011, dozens of mortar shells have landed on Israel's side of the Golan. There is no reason for that – unless al Qaeda wants to draw Israel into the conflict. What would a perspective Tea Party supported President say about the events which have been unfolding? If al Qaeda were to control the Iraqi oil fields and the pipelines which carry Iranian and Saudi oil through Syria, where will America be when all it can refer to as oil reserves is represented by tar-like shale oil deposits?

Think about the ramifications of the events in the Middle East, when you see the news reports of candidates burning jet fuel hopping across the nation on their 2016 campaign tours. Think about the reserves-to-production ratio forecasts that we will have depleted those liquid reserves in the first presidential term of whoever is elected.

Ask yourself: How important was a computer glitch in what was basically a free-market insurance company listing exchange of offered policies and prices? How important was that glitch, when the President gets on Air Force One and burns more fuel in a few minutes than you use to both operate your car and heat your home in a year.

After you addressed that personal query, consider what the following chart tells us about the performance of the American economy under the Republican or Democratic administrations.

(From Washington Post, 2 December 2013):

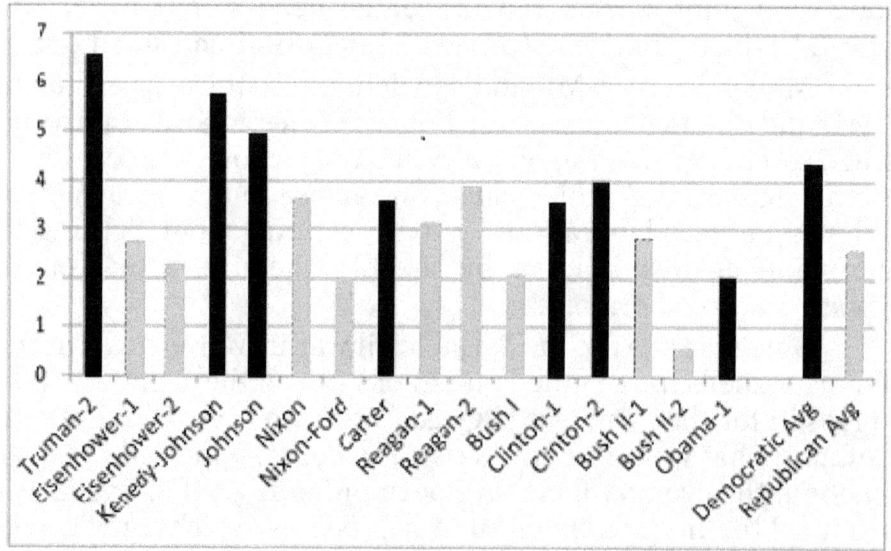

A. Average annualized GDP growth, by term

We begin with the fact that, since the end of World War Two, the American Gross Domestic Product (GDP), in real terms, has grown an average of 2.54 percent under Republicans Presidents and 4.35 percent under Democratic ones. Phrased another way, average GDP grow is near 78 percent greater under Democratic Presidents than it is under Republicans.

Three reasons are provided for the variance:

1. Oil Prices: The invasions of Iraq, and the disruptions which were caused, by Presidents George H.W. Bush and George W. Bush were far greater than the two OPEC-driven shocks under Presidents Richard Nixon and Jimmy Carter. However, these events will seem minor when we achieve anticipated oil reserve depletion and are totally dependent on foreign reserves. This would suggest the need for a normalization of relations with Castro's Cuba.

2. Productivity: Under Democrats, American productivity seems to grow faster. The biggest surges were during the Kennedy and Johnson administrations, but that also reflected the height of the baby-boomer era of creativity which, in turn, translated into the computer revolution. But that creativity was suppressed, and saw a brief, but sharp, downturn during the Reagan era in which grands for higher education were cut and the national debt doubled. Then, the first Bush administration continued that increase in debt, but the Clinton administration halted the debt hemorrhage, and had a surplus, which was squandered by the second Bush administration which again doubled the national debt.

In terms of debt and the squandering of resources by the Republican party, the Tea Party promise fiscal responsibility. That might mean they will strive to generate the Clinton era surpluses and the significantly reduce nation's debt burden.

3. Consumer confidence: It would appear that, whenever a Democratic President assumes office, the need to horde resources, or feelings of economic uncertainty, vanish. It would seem that, as no actual accomplishments can be attributed to the transition from one party to the other, people simply feel more confident under Democrats. Therefore we see business investments in fixed assets,

and increased spending on consumer durables.

While not deemed statistically significant, the real difference in the structural federal budget deficit under Republicans is about 47 percent higher than Democratic presidents over the same sixty-five year period, and, 2013, stood at $17 trillion.

Contrary to popular perception, military spending is seven times greater under Democrats than under Republicans. But, as military spending only averages about 8 percent of GDP, this does not drive the economic growth noted above. However, it give some basis to believe the Democrats are more security conscious – might be deemed more fiscally responsible on defense – than Republicans. With that fiscal responsibility emerging from the fact that they do not need to inflate the deficit in order to protect the nation. Again, one would hope a Tea Party President could duplicate this pattern.

It appears that, when Democrats leave office they leave an economy growing at 4.1 percent, the Republicans reduce that to an exit level of 1.8 percent. Despite the low growth rate inherited from the Republican administration, the first year under the Democrats is economically superior to the first year Republican showing. That said, neither party has planned, or made allowance, for government employee pensions, which represent a massive unfunded liability – how will the Tea Party solve this problem.

The reported statistics for the sixty-five year period studied seem to contradict Republican "Tax and Spend" accusations leveled at Democrats in their campaign rhetoric.

Given the statistics, Tea Party assertions of a desire to bring fiscal responsibility to government would seem to be aimed at traditional Republican candidates, and the old-line part machine.

Interestingly, it does offer an excellent platform for the Tea Party candidates within the Republican Party, and might well set the stage for a Ted Cruz nomination – assuming Cruz finds a means of overcoming the eligibility question. Failure to do so, prior to his actual selection as Republican Presidential nominee, would likely precipitate a Constitutional crisis which could cripple the nation.

How does that compare with their ten point platform?

Apparently, the Ten Core Tea Party Beliefs are (as published on their website):

1. Eliminate Excessive Taxes

2. Eliminate the National Debt

3. Eliminate Deficit Spending

Clearly, if the October Government Shutdown had passed on the final vote – had the majority had voted NO – America would have defaulted on its Treasury Notes, overnight the National would have vanished, and both the interest portion of the deficit, plus any related taxes, would have vanished. "Mission Accomplished?"

4. Protect Free Markets

Clearly a laudable goal. But how do you protect free markets in a world where many markets are closed, or controlled?

5. Abide by the Constitution of the United States

As we have seen throughout this book, this specific issue is the issue which controls its title. Setting aside the possible legalese which could be brought into play, is the Tea Party really going to honor the explicit words of the Constitution on an issue which is – on its face – rather clear cut? And, if so, when? Will the gorilla in the room pound its chest until the very last moment?

6. Promote Civic Responsibility

How does this play within the context of name-calling, or the putting of 800,000 workers out of work, and wasting $24 billion in Gross Domestic Product (along with associated taxes & salaries).

7. Reduce the Overall Size of Government

How is this accomplished in a forum where Congress cannot even pass a routine Federal Budget? If you cannot agree on what constitutes core spending, how do you trim the unnecessary?

8. Believe in the People

Make a clear, fact and evidence based case for an issue – 'God Said' type morality, or based arguments, have no place in law.

9. Avoid the Pitfalls of Politics

This is easy, don't play games.

10. Maintain Local Independence

The Issues 3

For orthodox Jews, it's called "Building a wall around Torah" and represents a basic set of assumptions: The first is the existence of a Deity – one that created rules we are expected to live by. Next is the idea that "it is better to be safe than sorry"; accordingly, if you are going to err, do so on the side of caution.

Do you really want to be in a position where you shave things too close and thus discover that everything is lost, or damaged to the point where the repairs prove more expensive than the few pennies you saved by shaving that extra bit?

For decades now, America has been experiencing debates predicated on the idea of all-or-none, or absolutes. The idea that we are going to run out of oil is ridiculous; never mind that you can breed traits in, or out of, any plant of animal, there is no such thing as evolution – the ability of nature, or a deity, to do the same thing, ior, better yet, create a system which does it automatically for the purpose of adaption to other changes.

Obviously no deity is smart enough to do something so complicated – never mind that illiterate farmers and pastoralists have been doing for thousands of years, no deity could create an automatic system to achieve the same end. That basic logic of the deity being stupid, or less competent than the lowliest man, is the absolute behind Creationist logic; they know the mind and abilities of a Creator deity far better than the deity, or evidence it provided.

When you 'build a wall around Torah,' basically you assume and accept the superior intelligence and reason. You also assume that, like a child being told by its parent to do something, you don't really need to understand why – when you get older, you will acquire the necessary knowledge and wisdom to understand the logic which prevailed at the time. Of course, with understanding, and any new knowledge you acquired, also comes the ability to alter what is, or was, traditional patterns of behavior.

Already mentioned several times, Climate Change is an issue which will come to the forefront of policy logistics facing each of the

Presidents who will emerge from and after the 2016 election. How do we 'build a wall around Torah,' when dealing with an issue like Climate Change?

First of all, the most challenging changes will be those which seem to be abrupt. But such abrupt changes will only come about if we close our eyes to what is happening around us.

Evangelicals – like Ted Cruz's father – are fully aware of the biblical warning in Matthew 24:42 "Therefore keep watch, because you do not know on what day ..." But, of course, you can never know the exact day of an event which only phrased in terms of other events transpiring first.

We know that atmospheric carbon dioxide levels are now a third higher than the highest level they have been in the past 3/4 million years. We also know atmospheric CO_2 levels work much like a transparent blanket, or thermal window, which is designed to keep heat in. The higher the CO_2 levels, the more solar radiation is trapped in the atmosphere and the warmer the planet will become – and as the Arctic icecaps melt, we can watch effect and calculate the long term effects, or time frame.

The biblical warning stems from the realization that most leaders tend to be short-sighted and are not looking past immediate events to see, or attempt to evaluate, the long-term ramifications of short term decisions.

We all have a tendency to do that; it is a basic characteristic of human nature, and a reason why those who can think long-term are often so successful. Looking at the short-term policies coming out of Congress, one wonders if there will be anyone in the 2014 race who will emit a sense of constructive long-term thinking.

As was noted, for Ted Cruz, evidence of long-term planning would have him immediately announce that he is ineligible for the 2016 nomination, and then begin the process of demonstrating he has solutions, that he recognizes the problems the nation faces and has devised ways to address them. Strangely, this means he must begin to act more presidential than his fellow Republicans.

It is only by taking the mantel of the anointed that there will be a chance the door will open for him to take on that role.

In the case global warming, Cruz would need to point to the decade of scientists monitoring the rapid declines in Arctic sea ice, and the reality that the rapidly warming climate has been putting increased extinction pressure on plants and animals. He, or anyone who wishes a position of leadership on a global scale, will then point to the pressure on ecological systems which support our agricultural industry and which humanity requires in order to survive.

Unfortunately that requires intellect and an ability to exhibit leadership in an environment of nay-sayers.

Over the next several years or decades, the planet is going to be warmer than most living species, including humans, have ever seen or experienced. Experts in the field are looking at a pace of change which is several orders of magnitude higher than has been experienced by any living species in tens of millions of years.

In religious terms, these events comport well with the idea of a post-judgement Garden of Eden emerging after a decimation of the global population – the cleansing of the infidels. Of course, the message which is used for the fundamentalists would need to be tailored in a way that reaches the secular community who comprise the voter majority demographic.

Given sufficient time, any species can adapt to change, and unless you are a Creationist, the evolutionary process is an accepted part of the history of the planet – and universe. But, given some geologically abrupt change, species have a tendency to go extinct. The political issue facing Republicans is whether or not they are the new Neanderthals and unable to adapt.

Other, more gradually occurring changes can still have abrupt impacts on the ecosystem and human systems, such as the loss of fisheries or shifts in where certain crops can be cultivated.

In the 1920's there was a fellow in Virginia Beach who was called 'The Sleeping Prophet' – most of his prophetic spoutings were little more than rehashes of popular mythology and scientific predictions for the twenty-first century. One such prediction spoke to the already noticeable gradual rise in sea levels, which Cayce phrased as resulting in an expanded waterway which would connect the Great Lakes to the Gulf of Mexico. Today he would be talking of shorelines being submerged and low lying nations sinking into the sea, and would sound no different than the scientists who are speaking of the global displacement of tens of millions of people which will begin sometime around the year 2050 – a time when the human population is projected to exceed 9 billion people, and the pressure on our food production capability will exceed capacity.

The Rapid loss of ice, due to global warming, would mean that sea levels rise at a much faster rate than the current trend, which would have the aforementioned significant effect on coastal regions. At this point in time, we are looking at a thirty to fifty year time horizon, with the bulk of the damage being complete by the end of this century – when the population is projected to exceed 11 billion people.

At some point in time, the Chinese one-child-policy of the 1970's, which is now officially a two-child-policy, will need to be imposed globally. American reproductive rates have already fallen below that statistical level, so the only political need is to address the anti-abortionists, who would see an unrestrained growth.

The next issue is one of what might happen if the melting icecaps caused the Atlantic jetstream to close down, or if there were large, rapid emissions of methane from ice and Arctic soil – though once considered possible, neither is now deemed likely to occur in an abrupt manner.

On the other hand, the acquisition of nuclear capability by nations with ties to al-Qaeda, or which are simply controlled by an extremist regime, could bring on events which would culminate in a *'nuclear winter'*. Aside from the immediate effect of starvation and disease – all *'The Four Horsemen of the Apocalypse'* type stuff that is so popular on cable television – the likelihood is that it would trigger a series of abrupt cascading changes in our climate.

But the question is, are there any politicians who actually believe in the biblical Apocalypse, or that "the time has come for us to quit talking and actually take some action"?

If a burst of fresh water were to enter the North Atlantic and dilute the ocean's saltiness, it would make it harder for cold surface water to sink; if that were to happen, the Gulf Stream (jetstream) would close down and Europe's source of heat would cease. This could happen if a nuclear winter were to cause the Bering Strait to freeze over. Why concern about a Pacific Ocean location in terms of an Atlantic Ocean system?

When the strait is open, water flows into the Arctic Ocean and eventually out into the North Atlantic. The Pacific Ocean water, is somewhat less salty than it's Atlantic counterpart. Melting water from Greenland ice only adds to the dilution, and thus gradually slows the system. Cut of the diluted Pacific flow, then sharply inject cold fresh water, and there is an abrupt shutdown.

In terms of the touted fiscal responsibility: According to a 2013 study by the American Meteorological Society (AMS) Policy Program, the maximization of returns on financial investments depends on our accurately understanding and effectively accounting for weather and climate risks.

In turn, short-term financial decisions exhibit the long-term implications previously mentioned, and in the United States' social and economic well-being depends, in part, on climate variability and change. As a result, given the increasingly competitive global environment, nations that invest most effectively with respect to weather and climate risks gain a competitive advantage.

How does this work?

In 2013, Colorado's northern mountain range had a drought which created the ecological environment necessary for a massive spruce beetle outbreak, which then impacts the lumber industry, and creates an environmental change which alter snow melt runoff patterns; in turn, this could affect flooding of low lying areas.

Predict a drought and you can predict an insect infestation outbreak. Predict that and you predict, and have the opportunity to mitigate, or accentuate, the economic impact. Deny climate change and you deny society the ability to profit from it.

If we look to the climate models available due to increased

computer speeds and power, we see that it is now believed that the in the period 2041–2070, the Midwest and Northeast will likely be more moist during the winter, and the western and southern states will face increasingly dry summers. What this means for population movements, or crops, is a matter for experts in those areas. But, 30 years is a full generation; children born in the first decade of that era will have children before it ends, and their lives will be forever affected by the experience.

Seven presidential elections, and three sets of policies carried across four Senatorial election cycles, and the lives of a generation will have been politically determined. But before we even get there, the next two election cycles will determine America's energy and economic future.

Congress and the Obama administration will, over the first eight months of 2014, make decisions with regard to raising the federal minimum wage, and with those decisions will come a lower public dependence on government largess.

If we look back on what the Obama Administration has done, it is a matter of record that Obama promotes pollution-free energy, and in his first term nearly doubled America's wind power as a way of combating global warming.

Unfortunately, green-energy has a downside which Obama's administration has not been able to address. It would appear that, in Wyoming, the Golden Eagle isn't intelligent enough to avoid the steadily rotating wind-farm blades. Of course, federal laws do not care if the birds are suicidal – the wind-farm are held responsible for any eagle deaths, or injuries. Obama's administration has been reluctance to prosecute such cases and apparently has helped keep the scope of the eagle deaths secret.

Are eagle deaths as significant as Obamacare?

Apparently not to the Tea Party. Or, more precisely, they would rather focus on stopping something which could potentially save the lives of citizens, instead of something which is a violation of law. There is no glamor in defending an Golden Eagle – it makes one seem like a tree-hugger. The last thing the Tea Party would want is to be associated with something supported by Democratic Environmentalists – yet that is how you win national elections, you cross-party lines on issues which are of national interest, or carry with them a vocal national constituency. Which is precisely what Obama did when he adopted the Scully Conservative Republican medical plan that the Tea Party is now attempting to undermine.

Obama appears to be doing the same thing by asserting the need for a higher Federal Minimum Wage.

Higher minimum wages are clearly not a Republican, or Tea party, issue. But the use of the concept *'A rising tide lifts all boats'* most definitely is.

Historically, it has been asserted that increasing minimum wages has the effect of lowering employment. But studies in Britain have proved that to be false. An increase in minimum wages seems to carry with it reductions in overall unemployment – as disposable income is increased, more goods and services are acquired, with an increase in employment and productivity commensurate with the increased demand for services.

A higher minimum wage along with the American Earned Income Tax Credit enhances employment and earnings for single women with children, which decreases portions of the burden now carried by SNAP and other assistance programs. However, it does have a negative effect on less-skilled male employment, but, overall, there is an upward movement for pay among the bottom 5% of all workers, which in turn has an overall positive effect for the national economy. Those in the know say, *'A rising tide lifts all boats, from beneath the hull.'*

As wage gaps shrink among the lower echelon, gender based inequalities fall, with the greatest effect being among the low-wage areas of the nation. This carries an interesting side-effect, as the wages are increased, employees seem to respond by working harder and employers invest in training and other workplace productivity boosters, with the result that there are more tax revenues generated.

Overall, the minimum wage becomes a win-win for the whole nation, including the federal budget and deficit. Thus we can expect that those who would see the nation bankrupted would also oppose any increase in the minimum wage.

Finally we come to the matter of distraction.

When you oppose positive taking action, or find you are bereft of constructive suggestions which would justify either your being retained in your current leadership role, or promoted to a higher level of responsibility, the ideal response is to distract.

Notice that Birthers also assert the need to impeach Obama for alleged lies, or statements, which they equate with meeting the Constitutional standard of '*High Crimes and Misdemeanors.*'

With less that a week left in the 2013 Congressional session, 13 of the 22 House of Representatives Republicans on the Judiciary Committee began to hint at, or threaten, impeachment of Obama.

Given that there are no actual crimes with which he can be charged, nor any clearly defined actions which would have resulted in the impeachment of any past president, the tactic becomes one of impeding the legitimate work of the House.

Vague accusations of "impeachable offenses", such as those leveled by Rep. Michele Bachmann (R-Minn.), create a smokescreen behind which the House Republicans can twiddle their thumbs until the 2014 election. Thereby avoiding their responsibility, for another year, to vote on and pass a Federal Budget, along with any and all of the meaningful reforms they assert would introduce a degree of fiscal responsibility into the governing process.

Rep. Trent Franks (R-Ariz) has said that Obama's actions "could be considered royal prerogatives, which is, if my history's right, what we had that little unpleasantness with Great Britain about." His statement provides a degree of comic relief for the 2016 election cycle – at least if we recall the words of Rafael Cruz taken from Proverbs 13:22, which was used to infer that an anointed 'king' (presumably a Republican) would emerge and then redistribute the wealth (a Socialist-Marxist idea) to the Evangelical backbone of the Republicans, or Tea Party Republicans.

But what wealth will there be, what will be available for their redistribution efforts?

Noting that the United States is the largest debtor nation in the world, and in history, in Dec. 2013, Jim Rodgers warned that Americans were floating around on a sea of artificial liquidity. One which was not going to last – possibly not even last past the 2016 election cycle.

Rogers claimed, "The next correction when it comes, because the debt is so very high — you know, 2008 was worse than 2002 because the debt was so much higher. You wait until 2015 or 2016 when the next crisis hits ... debt has gone through the roof, the next one's gonna be really bad."

That is a rather dire economic forecast, but one consistent with the October 2013 governmental shutdown and the fact that the final vote saw 162 Republicans (144 in House, 18 in Senate) voted to continue the shutdown and have America default on its lawful obligations. Thus we see that the Republicans have deduced that the road to fiscal responsibility begins with the defacto bankruptcy of America.

Were they Islamic agents, and adherents to the principals which govern actions by al-Qaeda, their vote would have been both logical and anticipated. Since 1993, al-Qaeda has asserted the goal of an American bankruptcy; they would also like America to be fully dependent on foreign fuel – in that way they can take control of Middle Eastern reserves, create an oil embargo, and thereby disable the American military. At that point, al-Qaeda would be free to expand throughout Europe, or Asia.

In 2014, the American voters will decide if they wish to vote for leadership which favors the average American, or the objectives set down by al-Qaeda. Though, in reality, many will simply abstain and accept whatever their fellow Americans decide.

One major issue will be the one which revolves around the concept of 'Traditional Values'. Whose traditions are to serve as a model? Does America declare itself a 'Christian Country', and if so, which form of Christianity is to define its values? Do we rely upon the Bible, or The Book of Mormon (which is purely American)? If the Bible, then what of the fact that no Christians actually follow it?

Tradition Values

The concept of 'traditional values' is often utilized to justify actions – but we are never told what those values really represent; whose traditions? The inference is generally that they are somehow biblical. But the reality is, those who hold up the book and proclaim its values are those who generally violate the specific rules which define those values.

The Tea Party, and the Republican Party, have asserted they stand for 'traditional values', but where do those values originate? From whose traditions are they derived?

Consider the "Defense of Marriage" argument – marriage is between one man and one woman. It sounds good and can be supported by the words of *Genesis 2:22-24*, "'For this reason a man will leave his father and mother and be united to his wife, and the two will become one flesh.' So they are no longer two, but one. Therefore what God has joined together, let man not separate."

Note the kicker, though it clearly asserts that the two shall become, that the union is between one man and one woman, there is a clear and irrefutable catch – they cannot be separated by any act of man. There is no divorce, unless commanded and sanctioned by God. Thus, if you wish to defend marriage based upon scripture, you must also eliminate divorce – a fact carried forward, and then affirmed, in *1 Corinthians 7:1-16*, where it clearly states, "A wife must not separate from her husband. ... And a husband must not divorce his wife."

Thus, if you assert traditional grounds for defining what a marriage should be, and the inference that your tradition is western scripture, you must also, with the same action, ban divorce.

But anyone who has read the Bible knows, it really tells us something completely different. Genesis is related to the Hebrew Covenant tradition, Corinthians relates to the teachings of Paul to the Gentiles. In *Mark 10:6-9*, the author relates his teaching back to the aforementioned verse from *Genesis* – thus binding, as Paul did, the New to the Old.

In ***Matthew 19***, we are reminded that speaking for God, Moses directed that a man could must give his wife a certificate of divorce (a Hebrew GET), if he wished to rid himself of her. But, once again, we find Genesis being sited – this time by Jesus – as the basis for there to be no divorce.

Those, in defending marriage, we can ask if those asserting traditions are asserting the Hebrew, or Christian. And, more important, are they asserting the values directed at the Jews to whom Jesus was speaking, or to the Gentiles who were addressed by Paul?

With regard to relations with their opposite gender, Jesus, in ***Matthew 19:12,*** is cited as teaching, "For there are eunuchs who were born thus from their mother's womb, and there are eunuchs who were made eunuchs by men, and there are eunuchs who have made themselves eunuchs for the kingdom of heaven's sake."

Thus there are three classes of eunuch, one practices celibacy in service to religion, another is made that way by an act of man, and the third are what we might call homosexual – it is how they are born, and today we know that five to fifteen percent of any mammal species falls into that group. Thus, like it or not, Christian tradition affirms homosexuality as being natural and outside rules pertaining to male female marriage.

Thus, these references indicate that the traditional values are the Hebrew ones which also condemn those who consume pork or shellfish – rules which neither Jesus nor Peter set aside, and which Paul mandated be fully adopted by his Gentile followers before they utter a single word against a Jew. There are the 'Traditional Values' which are presumably supported and used to justify the manner in which Marriage is defended.

But we still have the tradition derived, via Paul, for Gentiles.

Paul asserts they should be celibate, and if not, then married. He places no restriction, and, when the Roman Emperor married a boy, neither he, nor any of his successors, condemned the act. It was, after all, consistent with the lawful actions accorded to those "eunuchs … born thus from their mother's womb" who could not be celibate. A valid traditional value interpretation supported by a scripture which, despite that it was as common then as it is now, contains no law which pertains to homosexual behavior. Though it does contain one law – *Leviticus 18:22* – which prohibits male bi-sexuality. But, only male bi-sexuality. There is no corresponding verse for females, in a tradition which makes it a point to be clear if, or how, a verse that applies to one specified gender also applies to the other.

Thus we see that those who support divorce, or attack same-sex marriage, are apparently violating 'traditional vales' supported by scripture. Which infer their values are opposed to scriptural ones and places them among those of which scripture routinely warns believers to avoid.

Then too, if someone is an atheist – or an agnostic who does not accept the documents of organized religions – traditional values take on a completely different set of meanings. If they are followers of Islam, then the 'kosher' laws apply, but in a context of marriages which are more akin to that of the Hebrew Jacob, Rachel, and Leah – arranged marriages, and purchased brides, which allow a man to marry women who sisters, or cousins.

Abraham had his half-sister Sarah as a wife, and she gave him Hagar, her Egyptian handmaid – by whom Abram fathered his first son, Ishmael. If we look to the tradition vales of the Laws of Moses, we see in Deuteronomy 21 instructions based on acceptance that a man might have two wives:

"15 If a man has two wives, and he loves one but not the other, and both bear him sons but the firstborn is the son of the wife he does not love, 16 when he wills his property to his sons, he must not give the rights of the firstborn to the son of the wife he loves in preference to his actual firstborn, the son of the wife he does not love. 17 He must acknowledge the son of his unloved wife as the firstborn by giving him a double share of all he has. That son is the first sign of his father's strength. The right of the firstborn belongs to him."

If we study the 'traditional values' mandate, we see that the first born son – first male child fathered – has preferential rights not available to firstborn daughters or subsequent children; thus providing documentation of proper 'traditional values' which explicitly include polygamy and opposing them is clearly opposition to 'traditional values' outlined in scripture – and there are those who assert explicitly mandated by the supreme deity of humanity.

The Catholic Catechism, a 'traditional value' doctrine, tells us that Mary was a perpetual virgin; their canon, the New testament, also says Jesus had brothers and sisters – his brother John headed the Church in Jerusalem – which might explain the attitude of Jesus had toward polygamy: Joseph must also have had two wives. One can argue against it, but that would challenge the veracity of their 'traditional values' and go against what the Tea Party stands for.

Senator Ted Cruz identifies as a Baptist, thus he follows a doctrine which first appears in London around 1633 – making it a relatively new tradition, and one which arose concurrent with, or subsequent to, the founding of the Virginia Colonies. Thus voters could legitimately ask if his definition of 'traditional values' limits them to those established along with the American Colonies.

Again, voters must ask: What is the explicit meaning of the words 'traditional values'?

The oldest 'traditional values' revolve around family that is based upon polygamy. A polygamous Joseph raised Jesus in the orthodox Jewish traditions and the later religious mandates which Paul later stated would qualify his Gentiles as followers of Jesus. Those 'traditional values' require adherence to serving the poor and forgoing ones personal, or inherited, wealth in favor of aiding those who are widowed, orphaned, elderly, or sick.

We know that, when Jesus cited the Golden Rule, he was quoting the summation of Torah attributed to his teacher, Hillel. We also know that Hillel stated that Torah was the explanation of that rule. And we know Jesus didn't set aside the Laws, or Torah, he fulfilled them – just as Paul would later decree Gentile followers of Jesus would have to fulfill those Laws. That too defines the idea behind 'traditional values'; so can we believe anyone supports the concept of 'traditional values', if they do not adhere to Torah?

Or are they simply being dishonest – "Great Deceivers"?

Or are they talking different 'traditional values'?

In Islam, a man can have four wives; in the Hebrew he could have two – so long as he didn't prefer the children of one over those of the other. Then too, if he were a political leader, possibly a king, like David or Solomon, he might have a hundred wives. But those are also tradition values.

Since the American Constitution forbids the establishment of religion, it would also forbids giving preference to one religious tradition over another – especially if each divergent tradition was derived from the same one, and only varied by interpretation, or denomination. It is clearly illegal to give preferential treatment to one denomination over another, or to a derived variation over the version which constitutes the original parental mandate.

Isn't the assertion of 'traditional values', without specifying the tradition, an excuse for bigotry and discrimination?

Don't all legitimate 'traditional values' doctrines condemn such behavior – don't they condemn treating someone in a way you yourself would object to being treated?

Of course, 'traditional values' could also be a mediaeval idea that dirt protected from illness, and one should not bathe. It could hold that the poor are to be slaves, or belong to a class – or caste – that is to be looked down upon and abused.

'Traditional values' could favor nobility – the concept of a Messianic King who will rule the world, and bring an end to the idea of Democracy. Or we can have the ideas fostered by Rafael Cruz and his conservative followers. As we have seen, those ideas are predicated on an anointed king who will engage in a religiously derived Marxist-Socialist redistribution of wealth to his followers.

So the issue is, beginning in 2014, and over the foreseeable future, what are the 'traditional values' American voters will wish to have imposed their children, themselves and their nation?

When you hear the term 'traditional values', are you sure they are values you can live with, or even the ones you hold?

Congress - House

In July 2013, House Speaker John Boehner (R-Ohio) stated, "[Congress] ought to be judged on how many laws we repeal. We've got more laws than the administration could ever enforce."

In terms of limited government, the Nation has too many laws, and far too many which duplicate, or complicate other laws. To many agencies are dealing with the collecting of identical data before they can assist America's citizens, or direct them to necessary resources – be they informative, or licensing.

As Boehner asserted in an interview with CBS News' Bob Schieffer, "[Congress] should not be judged on how many new laws [they] create." They should be clarifying laws and addressing issues which benefit the people they are paid to serve, but in reality, they seem to be paid to take time off.

In 2013, the House scheduled 239 days off; they increased that number for 2014. Could you imagine any business which had its management vanish for 239 out of every 365 days – receiving about $1,400 for each day 'worked'. Those they are paid to serve are expected to put in 250 business days a year ibn order to earn the money, to pay the taxes, which pay the salaries of Congress.

Of the days in a year, 104 constitute weekends and 10 days are legal bank holidays; if we exclude overtime days, exclusive of their two week vacation, the average worker receives 114 societally designated days off. Even if we allow for twenty-five paid holiday and sick days, Congress still takes one hundred days more than those they work for. That's over three full months when they are neglecting the nation's business; yet they expect a generous lifetime pension.

The Tea Party asserts it stands for limited government, free markets, and traditional values.

Is it a traditional value to grant workers more free time than their employers, and also grant them larger retirement benefits – at the end of a few years of neglecting their duties and responsibilities?

The 2014 House calendar revealed members of Congress will only work only 113 days; in 2012 they only worked 107 days – which renders the Republican controlled Congress the least productive in modern history.

Given their past track record, how much less productive, how much more time can they spend avoiding the people's business, can we expect them to be after the 2014 election, when all 435 seats in the United States House of Representatives will be in play?

Will the American people elect another goof-off Congress to serve their needs until 2016, or will Americans seek people who are actually willing to do their jobs?

Have members of the Tea Party demonstrated a willingness to work, to actually address the problems facing America over the course of the next decade? If so, than, if elected into the role of a House majority, wouldn't they require a President who is conducive to their programs and agenda?

The Tea Party asserts their goal is fiscal responsibility, thus we can assume the rest of the Republican Party must shoulder the blame for the failure of the Nation to have a Federal Budget. If the Tea Party represents fiscal responsibility, then its members would have been on record demanding that both the House and Senate Appropriations Committees produce their budget proposals and ensure they are passed and forwarded to the President.

So why is the Nation operating without a Budget? Why is it being funded by Continuing Resolutions? How can any individual, business, or government bring its deficits under control, when it refuses to generate a budget, and persists in simply spending as if everything were an emergency?

Where is the evidence of fiscal responsibility on the part of the Tea Party? Of course they can blame others, but shouldn't they do so with clear evidence in hand that they did their part at every step in the budgetary process?

Whoever is elected in 2014 will need to first contend with the existence, or lack thereof, of a 2014 Federal Budget.

Of course, the immediate problem would be the fact that, for their first term, the President they are contending with would be Obama. Which, in terms of 2016, is actually an ideal situation for those who have constructive reforms designed to limit government and enhance fiscal responsibility.

In 2014, 33 of the 100 seats in the United States Senate will come into contention. That's fully one-third of Senatorial power, of that, half are currently in the hands of the 53 member Democratic majority – with two independents who lean Democratic. Therefore, a Tea party slate would only need to win six additional seats.

With control of both the House and Senate, the fact that the President is a Democrat and holds veto power, is irrelevant. In fact, in terms of the 2016 election, it is actually beneficial.

If, instead of taking a nay-sayer position on issues, the Tea Party were to show clear legislative leadership through the proposal of legislation clearly serves the interest of the people, while also limiting government intrusion into their lives and providing forward looking, fiscally responsible, answers to the problems which will confront the next President, any Presidential veto would serve their needs.

So long as the legislation is clearly presented – none of the "it bad", or generalized 'we're against', type statements – whoever stands on the Democratic ticket would be faced with the awkward problem of either denouncing a reform which is clearly warranted, or denouncing Obama and any Democrat who opposed the reform.

But that assumes there are rational reforms, and that the Tea Party is capable of demonstrating the ability to both recognize them, and provide intelligent solutions. Simply asserting a vague platform which favors limited government, free markets, traditional values, enhanced border security, and opposition to a healthy citizenry, is not going to set the stage for presidential office, or even carrying a Congressional majority in both Houses.

If anything, a failure to enumerate a clear, positive agenda, can only serve to negatively impact both the 2014 and 2016 election results. A fact that remains true, so long as the American voter does not seek to vote against their own long-term best interest.

The Babies

Since the 1990's there has been some debate about a link between abortion and increased risk of breast cancer. In many regards this has been considered a pro-life propaganda issue, but, in 2013, studies began to emerge from China which indicated there may indeed be a statistic risk factor associated with abortion.

If not for other known data, the Chinese data would indicate the possible connection might justify some women to avoiding the procedure and so avoid a greater risk of developing breast cancer.

The Chinese studies indicate a 30 percent increased risk of breast cancer. Looking at studies conducted around the world, it was discovered that two or more abortions might bring about a 76 percent increased risk, and three or more abortions apparently have a 89 percent increased risk.

The problem with the Chinese and global studies is the scope of the studies. Obviously the Chinese studies focused on Chinese genealogy, and we have no data on the genealogy of the subjects in the global cross-referenced data.

Oscar-winning actress, Angelina Jolie's mastectomy focused attention on the risks with being a carrier of the Ashkenazi BRCA1 mutation, which can bring with it an 87 percent risk of developing breast cancer. Television star, Christina Applegate also carries the mutation – though, in 2008, her breast surgery didn't garner the same level media notoriety.

The fact that mutations of the BRCA1 and BRCA2 genes have been linked to hereditary breast and ovarian cancer, opens the issue of whether or not there is some as yet unidentified genetic issue in Chinese women, or women in general, which is triggered by some forms of induced abortion.

The problem is, abortion often serves a solid medical need, and their denial, accompanied by the condemning abortions, while also denying women birth control, creates economic pressure points which are detrimental to society as a whole. As stated earlier, if any segment of a society deems it its right to insist that a child be born simply because a condom malfunctioned, than it has an obligation to see that the fetus and mother receive proper pre-natal care, a fully covered and qualified delivery, plus complete and appropriate post-natal care under a program which includes proper nutrition both mother and child.

As they insisted the child be born, they should also provide for its raising and education. But, as I type these words, I can hear them objecting to taking responsibility for their own actions – their insistence that their limited morality in light of a product failure be the law-of-the-land.

If they wish to assert 'traditional values' and hold that sexual activities outside of marriage negates coverage, so be it. But they still need to cover the an undesired byproduct of marital sex.

Of course, if they wish to assert 'traditional values', it should be noted that consensual copulation between unmarried individuals was, 'traditionally', the basis of a lawful marriage – there were no marriage licenses, registries, or any other requirements which in any way asserted a necessity for governmental permission to wed. Accepted tradition and practice held that marriage by copulation, or family contract, was legally binding and sufficient.

Interestingly, with all these differences, abortion was normal.

If we think about the Hobby Lobby case, basically a challenge to contraception, reality dictates the product will be abortions, or more pressure to expand welfare. But, the interesting reality is that the rates of pregnancy in the 12-44 age group have been relatively level since 1976, when Roe v. Wade changed the law; the same can be said for birth rates. But abortion rates have steadily declined – between 1990 and 2009, by 12 percent – reality, legalizing abortion brought about a decline in abortions. For teenagers, all numbers have fallen sharply (40-50 percent), a fact that can be attributed to a shift in when women are having their first child (late 20's to over 30).

If we think about it, didn't criminalizing alcohol increase drinking? Criminalizing drugs – which were, like Sherlock Holmes' ten percent solution, perfectly legal at the dawn of the 20th century

– created a criminal drug culture and industry. When something is legal, but regulated, the free-market criminal aspect of economic motivations to promote it simply disappear.

In the case of abortion, women are given time to think about whether or not they want to be mothers; moreover, they get to consider the negative effects of abortion. Also, where congenital abnormalities are a factor, they get the option to try again, as opposed to bringing a defective, soon to die, human into existence. But the long term evidence shows that those who are allegedly 'pro-life' are actually 'pro-hardship' – they seek to impose economic and emotional hardships on people they don't know.

Consider an issue they should be addressing – if they are really 'pro-life'.

Worldwide, about 5.6 million babies are stillborn or, every year, die soon after birth; roughly five percent of those deaths are accompanied by the death of the mother – about 260,000 deaths a year, only 1 percent are in developed nations, the balance are in the Third World. Where are the 'pro-life' groups, where do they spend, or squander, their resources? Certainly not in the Third World.

Simple medical care would prevent mothers from bleeding to death, or dying from infection, and also stop their newborns from suffocating. If the mother does manage to survive, she may suffer serious complications such as fistula, where tearing links the vagina with the rectum or bladder.

As most people know, the Supreme Court has legalized any abortion which is necessary to save the life of the mother. Those who are allegedly 'pro-life' are on record as demanding the mother be allowed to die – that saving a woman's life does not justify a late term exception to the no abortion rule.

The next two election cycles will, once again, be influenced by the level of intelligence, and moral honesty, of those who assert they are 'pro-life' but will pander to those who would see women die – would, in effect, have the government commit murder. Politically, these groups are no longer targeting the rights of teenage mothers, rather, they are attacking the rights of adult female voters.

Perception Problems

One hurdle is the way the republican Party handles problems of perception – the mismatch of their political assertions against objective reality. The year 2014 will see more data emerge, and, if it is utilized properly, that data will severely damage their standing at the polls.

In 2013, the most recent ***Programme for International Student Assessment*** (PISA) test scores were released, and they showed the American educational system – highlighted by the infamous, Republican, *No Child Left Behind* educational revamp, which has been utilized to cut funding from the very schools where additional funding is most needed – has proven to be an abysmal failure.

Granted, the United States has never been first in the world, nor has it even been near the top in terms of international tests. For the past sixty years, American students have typically scored at or below the median, and are no strangers to the bottom quartile.

It is well known that, during the same sixty year period, there have been serious efforts to promote thinking which is contrary to logic, and both observed or scientific reality – case in point would be a right-wing Republican push to teach Creationism in schools; as many are aware, Creationism an extremist religious assertion which holds that the *Book of Genesis* is to be taken literally, and all science is wrong.

However, those familiar with my [2012] book, **Genesis of Genesis**, know that much of the structure of Genesis – as defined by the Patriarch ages – is actually a calendar system which, though we have altered the associated mythology, we are still using. That book is also the first, and only, book to accurately and rationally explain the extreme ages of the biblical patriarchs in consistent and mathematically verifiable terms – linking Genesis to the architects of the pyramids and Stonehenge age megalithic structures.

Beginning roughly concurrently with the move to expand the teaching of Creationism in the public schools, International testing began with a study which tested high-school freshmen and seniors, across 12 nations, in the field of mathematics – an area of study which automatically adjusts for cultural and language differences.

The score for American 13-year-olds were significantly lower than students in nine other countries and ahead of students in only one. Another test, which focused on students currently enrolled in a math class, American students scored last of the 12 tested nations; when students not currently enrolled in mathematics courses were tested, America again scored last. We note that these students who were tested in the Kennedy administration, were a product of the Eisenhower administration's post-war educational policies, or lack there of.

A few years later, came the First International Science Study; American 10-year olds, who were exclusively the product of the Kennedy era school systems, scored ahead of all by the Japanese; 14-year olds, whose educations extended into the Eisenhower era, were roughly average; finally, those who were in their senior year of high school, and had their educational roots in the Eisenhower era, scored last of eleven international school systems tested.

A Second International Mathematics Study (1981-82), saw students in 15 systems tested, and covered 13-year-olds and seniors, and, on across-the-board, American 13-year olds placed around the median. With regard to American seniors, as reported in, *The Underachieving Curriculum: Assessing U.S. Mathematics from an International Perspective*, "average Japanese students achieved higher than the top 5 percent of the U.S. students in college preparatory mathematics ... the algebra achievement of our most able students (the top 1 percent) was lower than that of the top 1 percent of any other country." The education of those tested would therefore equally reflect Nixon-Ford and Carter Administrations.

Interestingly, when studies compared the per capita GDP with PISA performance, an article by Keith Baker asserted, "the higher a nation's test score 40 years ago, the worse its economic performance on this measure of national wealth-the opposite of what the Chicken Littles raising the alarm over the poor test scores of U.S. children claimed would happen."

The problem with the Baker analysis is the reality that, it is the parents, and not those tested, who affect, or create, the GDP per capita element of the comparison. Those tested reflect the current economy and the economy which will exist in the administration to be elected in 2016.

When three American states – Massachusetts, Connecticut, and Jeb Bush's Florida – were tested, the northern states were above *Organisation for Economic Co-operation and Development* (OECD) averages, while Florida failed in all but reading, where it was only average. If we ignore the testing, and focus on creativity as a source of per capita GDP, then we seem to be stuck with states that vote Democratic, and have a history of Democratic leadership.

Now these observations can be disputed – the pattern of naysaying, without factual substance, can be employed – but that would not alter the reality for the better.

We've mentioned SNAP, the Food program which basically underwrites low wages paid by many domestic American businesses – quite legally, given they are adhering to an outdated minimum wage scale. Curiously, fiscal responsibility would see Congress raise the Federal Minimum Wage to levels where food assistance would be rendered unnecessary for those who are regularly employed. If that could be achieved, the burden on the Federal Budget would be reduced. But that assumes a Congress that is capable of passing a Federal Budget, rather than operating via Continuing Resolution.

The change might not be major. In 2013, only 10 percent of those on SNAP were adults living in single-person households who were neither elderly, nor disabled and had no dependents. Fully 87 percent of recipients belonged to multi-person households which included either children, and/or someone who was either disabled, or elderly. The remaining three percent were part of multi-person households - possibly where one, or all, were employed.

When address households containing the elderly, or disabled, the matter of pension and disability compensation comes into play. The Congressional Budget Office has stated that 91 percent of all

SNAP assistance goes to families living at or below the poverty line, which is $11,490 for a single individual, $23,550 for a family of four, and $39,630 for a household consisting of eight people.

The average Social Security recipient receives $1,162.63 per month, or just under $14,000 per year for a 'traditional' elderly family where the husband were the sole wage earner and therefore sole recipient of Social Security benefits. For an elderly 'traditional' family of two, a husband and wife each over the age of 62, an income of $15,510 defines poverty; if they live Hawaii, $17,850; if in cold of Alaska, $19,380.

Based on these numbers, it might prove fiscally responsible for the Congress to vote an increase in Social Security benefits – thereby reducing dependents on SNAP and other poverty related programs. The might, in turn, reduce government payrolls and its future governmental health and pension obligations.

Curiously, the worst thing such and increase might involve is that some people would receive sufficient to increase their disposable income, which would then be spent in the local economy, and increase government tax income. As the expression goes, 'a rising tide lifts all boats, and it does so from the bottom."

The issue becomes, will any candidates emerge who promote rational fiscal reforms – ones aimed at introducing simplifications into government programs without diminishing their purpose?

A system in which benefits are denied, only to necessitate a replacement of benefits through a separate bureaucratic structure, neither limits government nor displays fiscal responsibility.

As with education, Republican politicians claim America has the best healthcare system in the world, but, as with education, the reality is that some thirty nations have better, cheaper, systems.

Until implementation of the Reagan-Bush-Bush-Obama ACA legislation was passed and implemented, America had the worst system of health care coverage in the industrialized world. Systems which are profit driven have an economic motive for employing clerks whose sole job is to find excuses to deny services, or any form of preventative care.

In terms of a free-market economy, with its focus on specific economic sectors, as opposed to the economy as a whole, denial of services and imposing economic restrictions makes provides a solid bottom-line logic. Unfortunately, such thinking undermines the broader economic base of a nation which relies on the long-term heath of its work force.

The current Republican leadership has no solutions to the problem of affordable care within a profit-driven system where it is advantageous to have policy holders who, after decades of making payments, quickly die of catastrophic illnesses which could have been addressed, or prevented, early in their development.

Unlike the average Frenchman, in America, only the very rich receive care from doctors who still make house calls – something which was the norm, when I was a child. Only the very rich, or the devastatingly poor, in America are unconcerned by co-payments, deductibles and coverage limitations (caps) which will drive them into bankruptcy when they get cancer, or any truly major long term disease. In America, it is not unheard of for a sick person to lose their home and life savings due to illness.

Catastrophic illness is a leading cause of personal bankruptcy in the America; it is also credited with necessitating termination of many marriages, where divorce a means of qualifying the disabled spouse for government benefits. The persistent insistence on the creation of policies which destroy families is hardly compatible with any rational 'family values' doctrine. The issue for 2014 and 2016 is the degree to which the electorate will vote against irrationality.

The eighteenth century German poet, philosopher, historian, and playwright Friedrich Schiller observed that, "Even the gods fight stupidity in vain." Over the three year period, beginning in 2014, and ending when the next President takes office in January 2017, the issue which will have been addressed is the degree to which stupidity has overcome those who profess a relationship with God.

Given the activities of Rafael Cruz and other Evangelicals, like it or not, there is a deity sticking its nose into a decision making process which will determine the out of the next two elections.

www.ingramcontent.com/pod-product-compliance
Lightning Source LLC
Chambersburg PA
CBHW070756290526
45795CB00002B/568